About this book

Harvard scholar Michael Hardt
Negri's major book, *Empire*, qu
it was published in the United
gans, such as the *New York Tin*
ing in terms of empire and im
other parts of the world – amc
disturbed by the book, feeling that it was analytically miscon...
undermined political resistance to imperialism, and ignored the
concrete experience and intellectual analysis of the Third World.

Atilio Boron argues that Hardt and Negri's concept of 'imperialism without an address', however well intentioned their commitment to human emancipation and a better world, ignores the
fundamental parameters of modern imperialism. Professor Boron
unpicks their arguments and confronts them with the social, economic and political realities of intensified capitalist exploitation in
today's world. Among the trenchant points he makes:

- The nation state, far from being weakened, remains a crucial
  agent of the capitalist core, deploying a large arsenal of economic weaponry to protect and extend its position, and actively
  promoting globalization in its own interests. It is only the state
  in the periphery that has been dramatically weakened – in relation both to transnational corporations and to core states and
  supranational entities like the US and the EU.
- Hardt and Negri are also wrong, he argues, in picturing production under globalization as disregarding national frontiers. This
  does not apply to labour, nor to cutting-edge technology.
- And their substitution of a nebulous 'multitude' for identifiable
  social forces and antagonistic social groups merely confuses
  political reality, as does their curious depiction of the super-
  exploited Third World migrant worker as a postmodern hero who
  is changing the world.

Boron concludes that *Empire* is a libertarian pessimist product
of the defeat of the socialist left in the 1980s and 1990s. Its authors
have abandoned social theory in favour of a poetic abstraction
which covers up the reality of a globalization process whose more
cynical apologists do not hesitate in presenting as a projection of
American power.

Critical praise for this book

'This is a powerful polemic, in the best sense of the word, against a currently fashionable book. But it is also more than that. Beyond his trenchant engagement with the arguments of Hardt and Negri, Boron offers, in accessible prose, his own insightful and eloquent analysis of today's "globalized" world and the possibilities of its transformation. The fruitful combination of theoretical rigour and clarity, empirical analysis and political passion is just the kind of thing we need on the left.' *Ellen Meiskins Wood, author of* Empire of Capital

'Atilio Boron mounts a severe, but necessary, criticism of the positions put forward by Hardt and Negri, who ... have aligned themselves with the attempt by intelligent rightwingers to neutralize the potential for popular mobilization on the part of movements supportive of a different kind of globalization.' *Samir Amin*

'The scope of this lucid and careful dissection of widely held beliefs about the emerging world order extends well beyond the influential study that is its immediate target. Boron strips away layer after layer of misunderstanding concerning "old imperialism" and its current variants. He reviews the persistence of the drive to control natural resources, the reliance of transnational firms on a powerful home state, the dangers of avoiding political economy, and much else. He brings out clearly the need for "an adequate social cartography of the field" where an "emancipatory battle" must be waged if it is to have any hope of success. In a critique of common illusions about contemporary society, Boron identifies and stresses the significance of social forces that have emerged and are engaged in the classic struggles that constantly take new forms, but reflect much the same deeper institutional factors and conflicting interests. This valuable study develops an important perspective on present realities and on what must be done to carry forward past achievements in emancipation from injustice, oppression, and degradation.' *Noam Chomsky*

'It is highly appropriate that the most trenchant and devastating critique of Hardt and Negri's mistaken and confused notions of a deterritorialized and decentered Empire should have come from one of the most creative and committed socialist intellectuals in the continent that has had the most first-hand experience of the actual workings of American imperialism. Writing in the tradition of – and in the process doing much to revive – the Latin American debates on dependency, neo-colonialism and imperialism of the 1970s, Boron not only confronts Hardt and Negri's abstractions with 'the prosaic Latin American contemporary reality', but subjects their work to a profound theoretical and empirical refutation. Written with exceptional verve and often biting humour, this is a book that especially deserves to be read by all those activists who, as Boron aptly notes in the preface to this new English edition, have been influenced by Hardt and Negri's 'severe mistakes of diagnosis and interpretation, which, if accepted by the groups and organizations that today are trying to defeat imperialism, could become the cause of new and long-lasting defeats.' *Leo Panitch, Co-Editor,* Socialist Register; *Canada Research Chair in Comparative Political Economy and Distinguished Research Professor of Political Science, York University, Canada*

About the author

Atilio A. Boron is Executive Secretary of the Latin American Council of Social Sciences (CLACSO) and Professor of Political Theory at the University of Buenos Aires. He was educated in Argentina and Chile, before doing his doctoral degree at Harvard in the United States. He has taught at some of the most important academic institutions in Argentina, Brazil, Chile, Mexico and Puerto Rico. In the United States he has been a visiting professor at the universities of Columbia, MIT, Notre Dame and UCLA, and in Britain has lectured at Warwick and Bradford universities. He is the author or editor of nine books (in a number of languages), including *State, Capitalism and Democracy in Latin America* (1995). His particular interest is the relationship between states, markets and democracy during the process of neo-liberal restructuring. In 2004 he was awarded the Casa de las Americas Prize for *'Empire' and Imperialism.*

ATILIO A. BORON

Empire and imperialism

A critical reading of Michael Hardt
and Antonio Negri

translated by Jessica Casiro

Zed Books
LONDON · NEW YORK

Empire *and imperialism: a critical reading of Michael Hardt and Antonio Negri* was first published by Zed Books Ltd, 7 Cynthia Street, London N1 9JF, UK and Room 400, 175 Fifth Avenue, New York, NY 10010, USA in 2005.

www.zedbooks.co.uk

Cover designed by Andrew Corbett
Set in Arnhem and Futura Bold by Ewan Smith, London
Printed and bound in Malta by Gutenberg Press Ltd

Distributed in the USA exclusively by Palgrave Macmillan, a division of St Martin's Press, LLC, 175 Fifth Avenue, New York, NY 10010

A catalogue record for this book is available from the British Library.
US CIP data are available from the Library of Congress.

ISBN 1 84277 576 6 cased
ISBN 1 84277 577 4 limp

Contents

Acknowledgements

A number of people have read all or part of the manuscript, making possible the completion of this book. Special thanks are due to Ivana Brighenti, Florencia Enghel, Jorge Fraga, Sabrina González, Bettina Levy, Miguel Rossi, José Seoane, Emilio Taddei and Andrea Vlahusic for their encouragement, comments and criticism. Jessica Casiro did a superb job of translating the rather baroque original Spanish into an austere but still lively English. Of course, none of them should be blamed for the errors and shortcomings of the book, caused entirely by the stubbornness of its author.

Preface

First, a little bit of history. In September 2001, one of the editors of *New Left Review* invited me to contribute a chapter to a collection of essays to be published by Verso in London. The book was to contain a series of critical commentaries about *Empire* by Michael Hardt and Antonio Negri (2000); their response would be added later.[1] Given that my contribution reached inordinate proportions, it was clear that it could not be included in that book. Far from being discouraged, I realized that the work I had already done, considering the importance of the theme, deserved a fresh start, so, after broadening some analyses, enlarging on a few comments, adding new data and new reflections, the result was this book.

What is related in the previous paragraph is the result of history and circumstances. There were also more important reasons that inspired me to write my book. First, there was the need to consider very seriously the work of two scholars of the intellectual calibre of Michael Hardt and Antonio Negri. Their intellectual and political trajectories, so broad and prolific, especially in the case of the latter, make them deserving of respect and for that reason I examined very carefully the assertions they made throughout *Empire*, a polemic that had such a strong public impact. Second, the subject matter of this book is of great importance: the empire, or, to use a definition that seems to me more appropriate, the imperialist system in its current phase.

The difficulties in undertaking such a task are many. I share the authors' critical view of capitalism and neoliberal globalization,

---

1 The book appeared, after considerable delay, in 2003 without the final chapter by Hardt and Negri. See Balakrishnan (2003).

and applaud their courage in examining such a crucial topic. In fact, no matter how deeply I disagree with Hardt and Negri's interpretations, I must admit that their revision and update of the subject were necessary both because the deficiencies of conventional analyses of the left with regard to the transformations experienced by imperialism over the last twenty-five years had become impossible to ignore and needed urgent updating, and because the shortcomings of the *'pensée unique'* on this matter – spread *urbi et orbi* by the IMF, the World Bank and the ideological agencies of the imperial system – to which the neoliberal theory of globalization gives expression, are even greater. For those like the writer of this book, to whom the fundamental mission of both philosophy and political theory is to change the world and not just to interpret it (to cite the well-known 'Thesis on Feuerbach' by Marx), a correct theory constitutes an invaluable tool with which the popular movements that resist neoliberal globalization can navigate, with a reasonable amount of accuracy, through the troubled waters of contemporary capitalism. One of the main factors inspiring this book is my strong belief that Hardt and Negri's response to this challenge is highly unsatisfactory, and that it could lead to new political defeats.

It is evident that a phenomenon such as today's imperialism – its structure, its logic of functioning, its consequences and its contradictions – cannot be adequately understood from a close reading of classic texts by Hilferding, Lenin, Bukharin and Rosa Luxemburg. This is not because they were wrong, as the right loves to claim, but because capitalism is a changing and dynamic system that, as Marx and Engels wrote in the *Communist Manifesto*, 'constantly revolutionizes itself'. Therefore, we cannot understand early twenty-first-century imperialism by reading *only* those authors, but neither can we understand it *without* them. The goal is to move forwards in a reformulation that, departing from the Copernican revolution produced by Marx's work, which provides us with an interpretative clue that is essential for explaining capitalist society, will reinterpret with audacity and creativity the classical heritage of studies on imperialism in the light of the transformations of the present. Today's imperialism is not the same as the one that existed thirty years ago; it has changed, and in some ways the change has been very important, but it has not changed into its opposite, as neoliberal mystification suggests, giving rise to a 'global' economy in which we are all 'interdependent'. It still exists, and it still oppresses peoples and nations and creates pain, destruction and death. In spite of the changes, it still keeps its identity and structure, and it still plays the same historical role in the logic of the global accumulation of capital. Its mutations, its volatile and dangerous combination of persistence and innovation, require the construction of a new framework that will allow us to capture its present nature.

This is not the place to examine different theories about imperialism. Let us say, to sum up, that the fundamental features of imperialism, pointed out by the classical authors at the time of the First World War, remain unchanged in their essentials given that imperialism is not an ancillary feature of contemporary capitalism or a policy implemented by some states, but a new stage in the development of this mode of production whose fundamental traits have persisted to the present day. This new stage is characterized, now even more than in the past, by the concentration of capital, the overwhelming predominance of monopolies, the increasingly important role played by financial capital, the export of capital and the division of the world into different 'spheres of influence'. The acceleration of globalization that took place in the final quarter of the last century, instead of weakening or dissolving the imperialist structures of the world economy, magnified the structural asymmetries that define the insertion of the different countries in it. While a handful of developed capitalist nations increased their capacity to control, at least partially, the productive processes at a global level, the financialization of the international economy and the growing circulation

3

of goods and services, the great majority of countries witnessed the growth of their external dependency and the widening of the gap that separated them from the centre. Globalization, in short, consolidated the imperialist domination and deepened the submission of peripheral capitalisms, which became more and more incapable of controlling their domestic economic processes even minimally. The continuity of the fundamental parameters of imperialism, not so much of its phenomenology, is ignored throughout Hardt and Negri's work, and this negation is what they have called 'empire'. What I seek to demonstrate here is that, in the same way that the walls of Jericho did not collapse because of the sound of Joshua and the priests' trumpets, the reality of empire does not fade away when confronted by the fantasies of philosophers.

The fact that Hardt and Negri's work appeared at a time when the periphery's dependency and the imperialist domination have grown to levels previously unknown in history is not a minor detail. This is why the need to have a renovated theoretical toolbox with which to understand imperialism and fight against it is more urgent than ever. It will be very hard to win this battle without a clear understanding of the nature of the phenomenon. It is precisely because of this need to know that *Empire* has had such an extraordinary impact on the large masses of young, and not so young, people who from Seattle on have mobilized throughout the world to put an end to the systematic genocide that imperialism is committing in the countries of the capitalist periphery, to social regression, and to the disenfranchisement that is taking place to a similar extent in both the most advanced and the most backward societies, to the criminal destruction of the environment, to the degradation of democratic regimes restrained by the tyranny of markets and the militarism that, following the attacks on the World Trade Center and the Pentagon, has permeated the White House and other privileged places in which decisions affecting the lives of millions of people are made. Despite the noble intentions and intellectual and political honesty of our authors, about which I have no doubt, their book – regarded by many as the 'Twenty-first Century's Communist Manifesto' or as a revived 'Little Red Book' for the so-called 'globalphobics' – contains serious mistakes in terms of diagnosis and interpretation which, if accepted by groups and organizations trying to defeat imperialism, could become the intellectual cause of new and long-lasting defeats, and not only in the theoretical arena. This is why I have attempted to put forward my critiques and to face the costs and risks entailed in criticizing a book which, for several reasons, has become an important theoretical reference for the movements critical of neoliberal globalization. I believe that a sincere debate about the theses developed in *Empire* can be a powerful antidote to such worrying possibilities.

Buenos Aires, March 2002

Prologue to the English-language edition

This book seeks to debate, both from a theoretical standpoint and in the light of the lessons provided by historical and contemporary experience, the theses that Michael Hardt and Antonio Negri develop in *Empire* (2000). While in previous editions I have chosen not to examine some events that were both momentous and spectacular, such as the atrocious 9/11 attacks in New York and Washington – although they seriously challenged the core of Hardt and Negri's theoretical argument – at present such an attitude is not only impossible but also undesirable. Indeed, the Iraq war has had the same effect on the analysis proposed in *Empire* as the collapse of the Twin Towers had on American self-confidence.

Much water has flowed under the bridge and much blood has been shed as a consequence of the persistence of imperialist policies since the original publication of *Empire and Imperialism* in Spanish in 2002. It is necessary, therefore, to render an account of these new realities. If, in writing it, my original idea had been to create a 'living text', to employ Antonio Gramsci's felicitous expression, the book could hardly remain impervious to the vicissitudes of a period like ours, characterized by infinite horror and terror dealt against defenceless populations – an infinite war or, as Gore Vidal suggested, a perpetual war waged allegedly in pursuit of perpetual peace – and by the unrestrained aggression against human society and nature perpetrated in the name of corporate profits and stock exchange prices. These villainies are called, with unparalleled cynicism, 'humanitarian wars' fought to build a more secure, peaceful and just world by characters as notorious as the Bushes, Aznars, Blairs and Berlusconis who today command the heights of the core capitalist states. Through the macabre manipulation of words and the systematic misinformation incessantly reproduced by the mass media, almost all of which is under the steely control of capital, their technologically ultra-sophisticated terrorism appears as regrettable but unavoidable 'collateral damage' and their wars of pillage and conquest become noble crusades in favour of freedom and democracy.

The object of this Prologue, therefore, is to present some theories regarding the characterization of the current phase of imperialism in the light of the lessons arising from the new epoch inaugurated by the events of 9/11 and, in particular, by the Iraq war. Such a revision is essential not only to foil the propaganda orchestrated by Washington and projected worldwide in relation to the US military occupation of that country, but because, as we shall see in the following pages, even within the ranks of the left an unfortunate confusion prevails with regard to imperialism and the forms in which it currently manifests itself. A confusion that is made worse by the malignant trend among a sizeable majority of progressive intellectuals to be 'politically correct' or, as the Spanish playwright Alfonso Sastre said, to be 'well thinking', that is, to abstain from challenging the dominant silent premises of our age which, as Marx and Engels discovered in their early texts, are none other than the ideas of the dominant class.

Given that without an accurate analysis of reality there cannot be a correct political line for combating the scourges of imperialism, clearing up this matter turns into an issue of the greatest importance. This Prologue seeks to add its humble contribution to that undertaking.

The 'harsh rebuttals' of the war in Iraq

Let us begin by paraphrasing an expression employed by Norberto Bobbio, 'the harsh rebuttals of history', to refer to the refutation, according to his analyses, of the Marxist theory of the state owing to the changes experienced by democratic capitalisms during the twentieth century. The military occupation of Iraq, declared by Washington with the support of its main client government, the United Kingdom, and of its luckily short-lived Spanish lackey, José M. Aznar, has in due course generated an extremely harsh refutation of the ambitious theorizations of Michael Hardt and Antonio Negri that are the object of this book. The events that unfolded in the international arena after the publication of *Empire* in 2000 have incontrovertibly refuted, with the forcefulness of historical fact, the rash theories they propose in their book. The latter not only proved itself incapable of adequately interpreting the history of imperialism and its current structure, but also of accounting for the defining features of the new phase begun after the collapse of the Soviet Union and the end of the post-war world order.

An examination of some of the main 'theoretical victims' of recent epoch-making events would include the following items.

1 *Hardt and Negri's conception of the role of the United Nations and international law.* As pointed out *in extenso* in this book, the authors of *Empire* grossly exaggerate the importance of the United Nations and international law. Lacking the theoretical instruments necessary to allow them to perceive all the nuances and complexities of the structure of the imperialist system – since such instruments are not to be found in the 'toolbox' of French postmodern philosophy, Italian politics and US economic science, the authors' three acknowledged sources of inspiration – they naively take for granted the 'democratic' appearance of multilateralism and of the United Nations system. They consequently confuse the empty formalities of the empire with its constitutive matter, thus mistaking form for substance. The contrast between this image and reality is evident even to beginners in the study of international relations. Blinded by the inadequacies of their faulty theoretical framework, once again transformed into a veritable prison for thought, Hardt and Negri are unable to see what was evident to everybody else: the invasion unilaterally

8

decreed by President George W. Bush caused the contradiction between their theorization and reality to become as glaring as it was unsustainable. Violating the alleged order embodied in the United Nations and international law, the United States decided – as official policy rather than as a position paper circulating surreptitiously in Washington, written by some paranoid hawk in the Pentagon – to ignore any resolution to the contrary that the Security Council might adopt, not to mention the General Assembly, and invade Iraq. Faithful to that attitude, the White House did not hesitate to move to the defence of its supposedly threatened national security, ignoring both the need to build laborious political agreements as required by the United Nations Charter and the need to submit to the dictates of international legislation that it had always considered to be a mere tribute to demagogy and that needed to be obeyed only in so far as it did not affect Washington's interests. This position was adopted even despite its high political costs, such as the rupture of the North Atlantic consensus, the crisis in NATO and the serious altercation with France and Germany, the after-effects of which will be visible for a long time. After the aggression against Iraq had been carried out, the Security Council unanimously adopted a resolution in October 2003 calling for the democratic and shared reconstruction of that country, but this was merely a *post bellum* legitimization of imperialist aggression that had destroyed the tottering remnants of the post-war order. As Perry Anderson poignantly observed, this unanimous vote in which the Security Council solemnly welcomed the puppet government established by the White House in Iraq as the incarnation of Iraqi sovereignty, while calling on the patriotic resistance movements against the invasion to cease their activities, bestowed the official blessing of the United Nations' highest authority on the American take-over of Iraq (Anderson 2004: 51–2). This resolution, however, was wrongly interpreted by Antonio Negri in a recent interview as proof of US capitulation to the United Nations, when it was exactly

9

the opposite: the impotent resignation of the UN in the face of the brutal outrage committed by Washington (Cardoso 2003).

Yet, the absurdity of this interpretation – admittedly, always difficult – of the current situation is also repeated throughout *Empire* in its interpretation of the past. This dangerous tendency to confuse rhetoric and reality led the authors, for example, to exalt the figure of President Woodrow Wilson in accordance with the most conventional ideological elements of America's establishment creed that present him as an 'idealist', an amicable and tireless builder of peace and a man inspired by the noblest Kantian ideas of universal community. In their own words, Wilson 'adopted an internationalist ideology of peace as an expansion of the constitutional conception of network power' (p. 174). This vision ignores, among other things, the acid remarks made by John Maynard Keynes about the duplicity and hypocrisy that Wilson exhibited at the Paris Peace Conference after the First World War, which led the English economist to conclude that the American president was 'the greatest fraud on earth' (Panitch and Gindin 2004: 12). Or to disregard the fact, in no way trivial, that it was during Wilson's presidency that marines occupied the Mexican port of Veracruz and invaded Nicaragua and the Dominican Republic, surely to help the locals gain a better understanding of Kant's *Perpetual Peace*.

2 *The conception of the supposedly de-territorialized and de-centred character of imperialism.* Another of the victims of the Iraq war has been the proposition that declared the obsolescence of territorial – and to a great extent material – issues in favour of the virtual, symbolic and immaterial. This volatilization of the territorial elements of imperialism (and of capitalism) allegedly results in several inevitable consequences: first, the irreversible displacement of ancient sovereignties, based on archaic territorial nation-states, by a 'smooth', supposedly supranational space, a place where a new imperial sovereignty would be devoid of any vestiges of links with national states and, therefore, of

any territorial or geographical reference. Second, the gradual disappearance of a territorially located centre that 'organizes' the international structure of domination. Given the former, the classic distinction between centre and periphery, North and South, vanishes into thin air. Instead of this, what would allegedly characterize the empire would be the primacy of a global logic of domination overcoming traditional national interests whose bellicose reaffirmation caused innumerable 'imperialist' wars in the past. Thank God, this period is now over!

If one thing was demonstrated by the aggression unleashed against Iraq, and before that in Afghanistan, it was the merely illusory character of these conceptions so dear to the authors of *Empire*, which Bush refuted with the rude manners of a Texas cowboy. One of the first readings that we can make of the events in Iraq is that (*pace* Hardt and Negri) the United States has fully assumed its condition as the imperialist superpower, and not only does not attempt to hide that condition, as happened in the past, but even boasts of it. It intervened militarily in Iraq, as it will surely do elsewhere, serving the grossest and pettiest defence of the interests of the conglomerate of gigantic oligopolies that form the dominant class in the USA, interests which, thanks to the alchemy of bourgeois hegemony, have been miraculously transformed into the national interests of the United States. It would be possible now to paraphrase the old motto of General Motors by saying that, in the current imperialist phase, 'What is good for the US corporations is good too for the United States'. The oilmen who today feel at home in the Oval Office pounded, with absurd pretexts, a country to take possession of the enormous wealth it harbours in its subsoil. Plainly put, the military occupation of Iraq is essentially a territorial conquest for plunder carried out by the main actor of the imperialist structure of our time under the pretext of preventing the deployment of yet unfound weapons of mass destruction and of avenging the even less likely collaboration of the Saddam regime with the former US mercenary Osama

Bin Laden. To conclude: there is nothing 'de-territorialized' or immaterial there. It is the old practice of conquest and plunder repeated for the umpteenth time by the same old actors wearing new costumes and showing some technical innovations. Essentially, it is the same time-honoured imperialist story.

Nothing, therefore, can be more inaccurate than the image evoked by Hardt and Negri in their book in which Washington becomes militarily involved all over the world in response to a universal clamour for the imposition of international justice and legality. A plethora of far-right publicists – especially Robert Kagan and Charles Krauthammer – have emerged into public view to justify this reaffirmation of an imperialist unilateralism which cares little or nothing for international justice and legality, joining forces with other authors such as Samuel P. Huntington and Zbigniew Brzezinski, who some years ago had already outlined the strategic imperatives of the 'lonely superpower' and the urgent need to take up the challenges posed by its role as the focal point of a vast territorial empire. One of those challenges, certainly not the only one, is the right – actually the duty, by virtue of the 'manifest destiny' that turns the United States into the allegedly universal carrier of the freedom and happiness of peoples – to go to war as often as necessary to prevent the fragile and highly unstable 'New World Order' proclaimed by George Bush Sr at the end of the first Gulf War from collapsing like a house of cards. And none of this can be done without considerably reinforcing the state-based national sovereignty of the USA and its effective organs of international operations, mainly its armed forces. This is why the United States' military expenditure has grown to almost half the planet's entire military outlay. Moreover, it should be borne in mind that, as Noam Chomsky has rightfully observed, the new American strategic doctrine announced by the Bush administration in September 2002 entails a plan to rule the world by force that has not been heard since Adolf Hitler made similar announcements in the mid-1930s, certainly not a minor detail

(Chomsky 2003a). In this way, the idyllic idea posed by Hardt and Negri – the United States giving up the defence of its national interests and the exercise of imperialist power, and transferring its sovereignty to a chimerical empire, for the sake of which the White House magnanimously responds to international requests for global justice and law – was buried under an avalanche of 'smart bombs' unleashed on Iraqi territory.

3 *A healthy imperialist dead body.* Another of the lessons of the Iraq war has been the updating of some of the features that characterized the 'old imperialism'. In the authors' version, the emphasis placed on virtual elements established an unbreachable frontier between the 'old imperialism' and the supposedly new empire, the former being understood as that system of international relations which fitted, approximately, within the canons established in Lenin's analysis and which to a great extent was shared by some classical authors on the subject such as Bukharin or Rosa Luxemburg. One such feature was, precisely, the territorial occupation and the pillaging of the natural resources of the countries colonized or subjected to imperialist aggression. From a reading of *Empire* there emerges a theoretical conception indifferent to the issue of access to strategic resources for the world of production and the sustainability of capitalist civilization itself, explained by the strong emphasis the authors place on the (nowadays undoubtedly important) immaterial aspects of the process of creation of value and the transformations of the modern capitalist corporation. Yet, the Iraq war, starting with its tragi-comical groundwork, demonstrated how inaccurate this conception was. We have only to recall President George W. Bush, with his quirky pathetic smile barely disguised, exhorting Iraqis not to destroy their oil wells and to refrain from setting them on fire, to understand the crucial importance of access to, and control of, strategic natural resources in the allegedly current world imperialist structure. Oil constitutes, at this time, the central nervous system of international capitalism, and its

13

importance is even greater than that of the world of finance. The latter cannot function without the former: the entire edifice of what Susan Strange has correctly labelled 'casino capitalism' would collapse within minutes if oil disappeared. And the latter, we know, will be exhausted in no more than two or three generations. It would constitute unforgivable naivety to suppose that French dissidence in the face of US outrages in Iraq is founded on the democratic and anti-colonialist convictions of Jacques Chirac or on the unquenchable desire of the French right to ensure for the Iraqi people the full enjoyment of the delights of a democratic order. What prompted French intransigence was, on the contrary, something far more prosaic: the permanence of that country's oil companies in a territory that contains the world's second-largest oil reserves. Against what Hardt and Negri induce us to believe in their sublimated – and hence complacent – view of the empire, one of the possible future scenarios of the international system is that of a heightened inter-imperial rivalry in which the sacking of strategic resources, such as oil and water, and the struggle for a new carve-up of the world could well lead to an outburst of new wars of pillaging, analogous in their logic although different in their appearances to those which we have known over the course of the twentieth century, in the days when imperialism enjoyed enviable health and was not dead, as they want us to believe is the case today.

4 *Another victim: the view developed in* Empire *of the erroneously labelled transnational corporations.* Indeed, Hardt and Negri endorse – unconsciously, I assume – the vision of the capitalist world assiduously cultivated by the main US and European business and management schools and the theorists of neoliberal 'globalization'. As is well known, in the thinking of the right the irresistible rise of globalization is a natural phenomenon as uncontrollable as the movement of the stars, and one that gives rise to a new world of interdependent economies. Economic agents therefore operate on a level field free of the obstacles previously

set up by powerful nation-states. In this space, free competition reigns, and the old asymmetries, with their hateful distinctions between metropolis and colonies, are a thing of the past, evoked only by leftists nostalgic for a world that no longer exists.

According to this interpretation, not only has there been a decline in the 'national' economies, devoured by the farrago of globalization, but large corporations have entirely sloughed off the last vestiges of their national ascription. Now they are all transnational and global, and what they require to operate efficiently is a worldwide space freed from the old 'national' hurdles and restrictions that might hinder their movements. Within a supposedly anti-capitalist reading this space would be the empire, precisely as it is characterized in the work of Hardt and Negri. As I shall demonstrate in the following pages, the reality is light-years away from this vision. There is an elementary distinction (completely ignored in the work under review) between the theatre of operations of the companies and the territorial space in which their ownership and control materialize. Even in the case of modern corporate Leviathans – a small proportion of the total number of companies existing in the world – whose scale of operations is clearly planetary, ownership and control always have a national base: companies are legal entities incorporated in a specific country and not merely registered at the United Nations in New York. They have headquarters in a given city, obey a specific national legal framework that protects them from potential expropriations, pay taxes on their income and profits in the country where their headquarters are located, and so on.

The *New York Times*'s conservative columnist Thomas Friedman scorned the Silicon Valley executives who like to say:

We are not an American company ... We are IBM Canada, IBM Australia, IBM China ... Then, the next time IBM China gets in trouble in China, call Jiang Zemin for help. And the next time Congress closes another military base in Asia, call Microsoft

15

navy to secure the sea lines in the Pacific. And the next time Congress wants to close more consulates and embassies, call Amazon.com to order a new passport. (Friedman, 1999)

In case this argument does not look persuasive enough to dispel the myth of the 'transnational' nature of the modern capitalist enterprise, the conduct of the White House in Iraq and its brutal insistence, with the uncultured manners of Texas ranchers, that the beneficiaries of the war undertaken in the name of freedom and democracy (and of the need to free the world from the threat of a dangerous monster like Saddam) must be restricted to US corporations (especially but not only Halliburton) demonstrate the mistakes made in the theses developed in *Empire*. Not only that. It is no longer simply an issue of US corporations obtaining the lion's share of the spoils of the Iraq operation; the very manner in which these privileges were distributed among companies all linked to the governing US gang recalls the methods employed by the families of the New York Mafia to divide up control over business in the city. What relation is there between this imperialist carve-up and the idyllic theorizations found in *Empire*? Absolutely none.

5 *Social movements opposed to neoliberal globalization.* Lastly, a few paragraphs are needed to examine the role performed by those movements opposed to neoliberal globalization that the capitalist press, and this is no coincidence, calls 'non-global' or 'anti-globalization'. The hardly innocent purpose of this semantic choice is more than evident: to transform the critics of neoliberal globalization into antediluvian monsters who seek to halt the march of history and of technological progress. 'Non-global' activists thus appear before the eyes of world public opinion as a multifarious set of melancholy seekers after Utopia in a world that, as Francis Fukuyama and George Soros have said, dances to the tune of the markets. Thrown together are socialists, communists, anarchists, ecologists, pacifists, human rights

militants, feminists, aboriginal organizations and all sorts of sects and tribes, who wilfully ignore the fact that for the first time in history the world has been 'universalized' following an American pattern, and for that reason the end has been decreed for all kinds of millenarianisms and particularisms. Yet, contrary to this biased opinion, the movements that resist the markets' tyranny believe that another globalization is possible (and urgently necessary), that the current one is the product of the, until recently, uncontested predominance of large corporations. Then, there is nothing natural about the current shape of globalization; it is the product of the defeat suffered by popular, left-wing and democratic forces in the 1970s and 1980s. History, far from having ended, is just at its beginning, and the current situation can and must be reversed.

The vigorous emergence of such movements contradicts some central planks in Hardt and Negri's book. The 'non-globals' have earned the huge merit of having launched a large pacifist movement even before the beginning of operations in Iraq. While, as Noam Chomsky recalls, pacifism in relation to the Vietnam War did not appear, and then timidly, until more than five years after the beginning of the military escalation in South Vietnam, in the case of the recent war on Iraq this movement managed to articulate massive protests of unprecedented vigour weeks before the beginning of hostilities. It is calculated that some 15 million people demonstrated for peace in major cities throughout the world. In Britain and Spain, countries ruled by governments complicit in US imperialist aggression, street demonstrations reached an unprecedented size. The governments of Blair and Aznar provided an exemplary lesson on the limitations of capitalist democracy by ignoring, with absolute cynicism, what the demos, the supposed sovereign of an allegedly democratic political order, demanded with its mobilizations and its answers to numerous public opinion surveys. As I have argued elsewhere, in democratic capitalisms what matters is the 'capitalism' component

17

of the formula; the 'democratic' part is merely an accessory to be respected as long as it does not affect anything considered fundamental (Boron 2002). This imperial pillaging was decided by the 'ruling junta' that currently governs the United States. Let us recall, with Gore Vidal, that Bush is the first US president to reach the White House through an institutional coup perpetrated by that country's Supreme Court – there was no need to be bothered by democratic 'formalities' (Vidal 2002: 158–9). The petty despots did what they wanted and continued with the plan drawn up by White House hawks, despite its overwhelming repudiation by the public. In Spain, over 90 per cent of those interviewed were against going to war, despite which the government of the Popular Party continued with its policy. The terrorist attack of 11 March 2004, and the shameful lies of the Aznar government, prompted his resounding electoral defeat. Noam Chomsky is right when he observes that, for Bush, Rumsfeld and their friends, 'Old Europe, the bad Europe, were the countries where the governments took the same position as the overwhelming majority of their population. New Europe were the countries where the governments overruled an even larger proportion of their population. The criterion was absolutely explicit – you couldn't say more dramatically 'I hate and despise democracy' (Chomsky 2003b: 29).

All the above is to the point because, in *Empire*, the authors celebrate as the real 'hero' of the struggle against the empire the anonymous and uprooted migrant, who abandons his or her homeland in the Third World to penetrate the belly of the beast and, from there and along with others who like him or her constitute the famous 'multitude', fights the masters of the universe. Without diminishing the importance which these social actors may have, the truth is that what has been seen in recent years – and especially in the demonstrations against the war in early 2003 – is the vigour of a social movement that has solid roots in the social structures of metropolitan capitalism and that attracts numerous supporters, especially although not only

18

among the young, from large social sectors that are suffering an accelerated process of decay by virtue of neoliberal globalization. This is not to deny the participation of groups of immigrants in such mobilizations, but the fact is that the social composition of these movements suggests that the presence of the latter is, more than anything, marginal. In any case, because of its complexity and radical nature, its original innovation as regards the strategic organization of collective subjects, its discursive models, its style of action and, lastly, its militant anti-capitalism, the 'non-global' movement represents one of the most serious challenges that the empire has to face. This likewise constitutes a new aspect that raises serious doubts about the theses drawn up by Hardt and Negri regarding the subjects of social confrontation and the uncertain sociological physiognomy of the 'multitude'.

To recapitulate

We are living at a very special moment in the history of imperialism: the transition from one phase (let us call it 'classical') to another whose details are only just beginning to be sketched out but whose general outline is already clearly discernible. Nothing could be more mistaken than to posit, as Hardt and Negri do in their book, the existence of such an implausible entity as an empire without imperialism – a paralysing political oxymoron. Hence the need to argue against their theses, since, given the exceptional gravity of the current situation – a capitalism increasingly reactionary in the social, economic, political and cultural spheres, one that criminalizes social protest and militarizes international politics – only an accurate diagnosis of the structure and operation of the international imperialist system will allow those social movements, political parties, labour unions and popular organizations of all types that want to overthrow the current situation to face new journeys of struggle with any chance of success. An accurate diagnosis is also needed to identify the empire's enemies. To consider, as Negri does, that Lula in Brazil and Kirchner in Argentina represent a species of resolute 'empire fighters'; or judging as 'absolutely positive' the first year and a half of Lula's government in Brazil, turning a deaf ear to the deepening of the neoliberal course of the economic policy implemented since his accession to the presidency; or assuring his readers that the Kirchner government has refused to pay the debt, an astonishing discovery for the Argentinians who every day read in the press the inordinate amount of dollars being punctually paid to foreign creditors – these are certainly not the best ways for intellectuals to help defeat the empire (Duarte-Plon 2004: 1).

The illusion that we can undertake the struggle without a precise knowledge of the terrain in which the major battles of humanity will be fought can only lead to new and overwhelming defeats. Dear Don Quixote is not a good example to be imitated in politics; confusing windmills with powerful knights with lances and armour was not the best path towards the realization of his dreams. Nor will St Francis of Assisi, another figure exalted in Hardt and Negri's text, serve as a model for inspiration. In fact, no emancipatory struggle is possible without an adequate social cartography to describe precisely the theatre of operations, and the social nature of the enemy and its mechanisms of domination and exploitation.

The distortions that result from a mistaken conception, such as is maintained by Hardt and Negri, can be astonishing. It is sufficient here to quote the latter when he states, among other things, that 'the war in Iraq was a coup d'état by the United States against the empire' (ibid.). I would like to conclude by quoting extensively from an interview granted by Negri to the Argentine newspaper *Clarín* during his visit to Buenos Aires, whose eloquence is unsurpassable. In it Negri avers that the current United States occupation of Iraq does not constitute a case of

colonial administration, but rather a classical case of nation building. And therefore it is a transformation in the direction of democracy. This is the pretext of the United States. It is a military occupation that toppled a regime, but afterwards the problem is nation building, in other words an attempt at a transition, not at colonization. It would be like saying that the fact of turning from dictatorship to democracy in Hungary or Czechoslovakia is a colonization. There is no attitude of that type in the United States administration. These Americans want to seem nastier than they are. (Cardoso 2003)

It is convenient to ask ourselves, in the face of this incredible confusion, in which a war of pillage and territorial occupation appears to have been sweetened into an altruistic operation of nation-building and the export of democracy: will it be possible to advance in the concrete struggle against the 'really existing' imperialism armed with such crude theoretical instruments as are proposed by these authors and that lead them to such nonsensical conclusions? Ultimately, to philosophize is to make distinctions. A philosophy incapable of differentiating between a war of conquest and the process of nation-building is a bad philosophy.

To advocate carefully the features of a new society will be to little avail without a realistic knowledge of the physiognomy of the current society that must be overcome. A post-capitalist and post-imperialist world is possible. More than that: I would say it is essential, because, if it continues to operate under the predatory logic of capitalism, mankind is heading towards self-destruction. But before building this new society – more humane, just, free and democratic than the preceding one – it will be necessary to employ all our energies to overcome the one that today oppresses, exploits and dehumanizes us, and that condemns almost half the world's population to subsist miserably on less than two dollars a day. And this true emancipatory epic has, as one of its most important enabling conditions, the existence of a realistic and precise knowledge of the world we seek to transcend. If instead of

21

this we are the prisoners of the illusions and mystifications that are so efficiently manufactured and spread by the ideological apparatuses of the bourgeoisie, our hopes of building a better world will ineluctably sink. This book seeks to be a modest contribution towards avoiding such a sad and cruel outcome.

Buenos Aires, September 2004

1 On perspectives, the limits of visibility and blind spots

Something that may surprise the reader of Hardt and Negri is the scant attention that *Empire* pays to the literature about imperialism. In contrast with Lenin and Rosa Luxemburg, who made a careful review of the numerous works on the topic, our authors have opted to ignore a great part of what has been written about the issue. The literature with which they deal is a combination of North American social science, especially international political economy and international relations, mixed with a strong dose of French philosophy. This theoretical synthesis is packaged in a clearly postmodern style and language, and the final product is a theoretical mix that, despite the authors' intentions, is unlikely to disturb the serenity of the moneyed lords who year after year gather in Davos. Due to this, almost all the citations are taken from books or articles published within the limits of the French–American academic establishment. The considerable literature concerning imperialism and the functioning of the imperial system produced in Latin America, India, Africa and other parts of the Third World does not even merit a footnote. Discussions within classical Marxism – Hilferding, Luxemburg, Lenin, Bukharin and Kautsky – about the topic are allocated a brief chapter, while the controversies of the post-war period occupy an even smaller space. Names such as Ernst Mandel, Paul Baran, Paul Sweezy, Harry Magdoff, James O'Connor, Andrew Shonfield, Ignacy Sachs, Paul Mattick, Elmar Altvater and Maurice Dobb are conspicuous absences in a book that pretends to shed new light on an entirely novel stage of the history of capital. It is not surprising, thus, that this enterprise offers a vision of the empire viewed from above, from its dominant strata. A partial and unilateral vision, therefore, unable to perceive the totality of the system and to account for its global manifestations beyond what, presumably, occurs on the North Atlantic shores. Thus, the resulting vision is particularly narrow, and the blind spots are numerous and important, as I will demonstrate throughout the pages that follow. In short, *Empire* offers a vision that wants to be a critical examination going to the root of the problem, but given the fact that it cannot emancipate itself from the privileged place from where it observes the social scene of its time – the opposite of what occurred with Marx who, from London, knew how to detach himself from that fate – it is trapped in the ideological nets of the dominant classes.

How can the negation of the role played by two crucial institutions that organize, monitor and supervise the day-to-day operation of the empire – the International Monetary Fund and the World Bank – barely mentioned in the almost five hundred pages of the book, be understood if not from the limitations of a North Atlantic perspective? Barely six pages are reserved for an analysis of transnational corporations, strategic players in the world economy, only half of the amount devoted to issues, presumably so crucial and urgent, such as the 'non-place of power'. The eleven pages devoted to Baruch Spinoza's contributions to political philosophy, or the sixteen devoted to exploring the meandering of Foucault's thought and its relevance to understanding the imperial order, can hardly be considered sensible for those who see the world not from the imperial system's vertex but from its base.

For this and many other reasons, *Empire* is an intriguing book that combines some incisive illuminations about old and new problems with monumental mistakes of appreciation and interpretation. There is no doubt that the authors are strongly

---

1 The page references are taken from the original English-language edition: *Empire* (Cambridge, MA: Harvard University Press, 2001).

committed to the construction of a good society and, specifically, a communist society. This commitment appears many times throughout the book and deserves enthusiastic support. Surprisingly, however, the argument of *Empire* has nothing to do with the great tradition of historical materialism. The audacity exhibited by the authors when, swimming against the tide of established prejudices and the neoliberal commonsense of our times, they declare their loyalty to communist ideals – 'No, we are not anarchists but communists' (p. 350); 'the irrepressible lightness and joy of being communist' (p. 413) – collapses like a house of cards when they need to explain and analyse the imperial order of today.[1] At that point, theoretical and political indecisiveness take the place of declamatory conclusiveness. In this sense, it is impossible to ignore the contrast with other works about the same topic, such as Samir Amin's *Accumulation on a World Scale* (1974), *Empire of Chaos* (1992) and, the most recent, *Capitalism in the Age of Globalization* (1997); or *The Long Twentieth Century* by Giovanni Arrighi (1995); or *Year 501. The Conquest Continues* (1993) and *World Orders, Old and New* (1994) by Noam Chomsky; or *Production, Power, and World Order* by Robert Cox (1987); and the works of Immanuel Wallerstein, *The Modern World System* (1974–88) and *After Liberalism* (1995). And the results of such a comparison are extremely unfavourable for Hardt and Negri.

2 The constitution of the empire

Empire begins with a section devoted to 'the political constitution of the present', which follows a Preface in which the authors introduce the main thesis of the book: an empire has emerged and imperialism has ended (pp. xi–xvii). In the first part of the book, the analysis of the world order begins in a surprisingly formalistic mode, at least for a Marxist, since the constitution of the empire is laid out in narrowly juridical terms. Thus, the world order, far from being conceived as the hierarchical and asymmetrical organization of states, markets and nations under the general direction of an international dominant bloc, is misrepresented in Hardt and Negri's analysis as a projection of the United Nations' formal organization. This surprise is then intensified when the intrigued reader realizes that the conceptual instruments used by Hardt and Negri to examine the world order problem are borrowed from such unpromising toolboxes as the ones used by a group of authors so foreign to historical material-ism – and of such little use for a deep analysis of this type of issue – such as Hans Kelsen, Niklas Luhmann, John Rawls and Carl Schmitt. Supported by authorities such as these, it comes as no surprise that the results of this initial incursion into the subject matter are far from satisfactory. For example, the United Nations' role in the so-called world order is grossly over-estimated: 'one should also recognize that the notion of right defined by the UN Charter also points toward a new positive source of juridical production, effective on a global scale – a new center of normative production that can play a sovereign juridical role' (p. 4).

Hardt and Negri seem to ignore the fact that the United Nations is not what it appears to be. In fact, because of its bureau-cracy and elitism, the UN is an organization destined to support the interests of the great imperialist powers, especially the United States. The effective UN 'juridical production' has little substance or impact when it concerns matters that contradict the interests of the United States and its allies. The authors over-estimate the very marginal role played by the United Nations General Assembly, where the votes of Gabon and Sierra Leone are equal to those of the United States and the United Kingdom. Most of the General Assembly's resolutions are reduced to dead letters unless they are actively supported by the hegemonic power and its partners. The 'humanitarian war' in Kosovo, for example, was carried out in the name of the United Nations but completely bypassed the authority of the Security Council and the General Assembly. Washington decided that a military intervention was necessary and that is what happened. Years later, George W. Bush Junior invaded and devastated Iraq without the authorization of the Security Council, not to mention the approval of the General Assembly. Naturally, that bears no relationship to the production of a universal law or, as Kelsen trusted, with the emergence of a 'transcendental schema of the validity of right situated above the nation-state' (p. 6). The imperialistic nature of the 'really existing' United Nations, not the one imagined by our authors, is sufficient to prove the weakness of the following affirmation: 'This is really the point of departure for our study of Empire: a new notion of right, or rather, a new inscription of authority and a new design of the production of norms and legal instruments of coercion that guarantee contracts and resolve conflicts' (p. 9).

This fantastic and childish vision of a supposedly post-colonial and post-imperialist international system reaches its climax when they conclude that 'All interventions of the imperial armies are solicited by one or more of the parties involved in an already existing conflict' (p. 15); or when they hold that the 'first task of Empire, then, is to enlarge the realm of the consensuses that support its own power' (p. 15); or when they assure already astonished readers that the intervention of the empire is 'legitimated not by right but by consensus' in order to 'intervene in the name of any type of emergency and superior ethical principles' such as 'the appeal to the essential values of justice' (p. 18). Is it the 'humanitarian' intervention in the former Yugoslavia that our authors have in mind? Indeed, as will soon become clear. This incredible nonsense allows them to conclude that, under the empire, 'the right of the police is legitimated by universal values' (ibid.). It is telling that such a radical thesis is supported by evidence provided by two bibliographic references that allude to the conventional literature of international relations and whose right-wing bias is evident to even the least-informed reader. The voluminous Latin American bibliography about imperialistic intervention produced by authors such as Pablo González Casanova, Agustín Cueva, Ruy Mauro Marini, Gregorio Selser, Gerard-Pierre Charles, Eduardo Galeano, Theotonio dos Santos, Juan Bosch, Helio Jaguaribe, Manuel Maldonado Denis, is ignored.[1]

The second chapter of Part 1 is devoted to biopolitical production. It opens with a laudable statement of intent: to overcome the limitations of the juridical formalism with which they began their intellectual course, descending, in their own words, to the material conditions that sustain the legal and institutional framework of the empire. Their objective is to 'discover the means and forces of the production of social reality along with the subjectivities that animate it' (p. 22). Unfortunately, such beautiful intentions remain mere declamations, as the invoked materialistic conditions 'vanish into thin air', to use the well-known metaphor by Marx and Engels in the *Manifesto*, and some venerable ideas from the social sciences are presented as if they were the latest

---

1 When this work was practically finished, an excellent book by Saxe-Fernández, Petras, Veltmeyer and Núñez was given to me but I was able to take only marginal advantage of its empirical and interpretative richness (Saxe-Fernández et al. 2001). In any case, the reader is recommended to consult that text in order to expand some of the analyses undertaken in this book.

'discovery' by the Parisian *rive gauche* or New York's Greenwich Village. Foucault's theorization about the transition to the society of control, for example, revolves round the supposedly new notion that 'Biopower is a form of power that regulates social life from its interior', or that 'Life has now become [...] an object of power' (pp. 23, 24).

It would not take long to find in the extended western political tradition, that begins at least in the fifth century BC in Greece, ideas surprisingly similar to what today, with the fanfare that supposedly celebrates great scientific accomplishments, is called the 'biopower'. A quick look at the literature would show dozens of citations from authors such as Plato, Rousseau, de Tocqueville and Marx, to mention only a few of the most obvious, that refer precisely to some of the 'great novelties' produced by the social sciences at the end of the twentieth century. Plato's insistence on the psychosocial aspects – summarized in the phrase 'the individual's character' – that regulated the social and political life of the Athenian polis is well known, as is the young Marx's emphasis on the subject of the 'spiritualization of the domination' of the bourgeoisie by the exploited classes. It was Rousseau who stated the importance of the process by which the dominated were induced to believe that obedience was a moral duty. This made disobedience and rebellion a cause for serious conflict within individual consciences. In short, for Hardt and Negri, who are dazzled by Foucault's (an author who deserves our respect) theoretical innovations, it could be highly educational to read what was written a century and a half ago, for instance, by Alexis de Tocqueville: 'Formerly tyranny used the clumsy weapons of chains and hangmen; nowadays even despotism, though it seemed to have nothing more to learn, has been perfected by civilization.' And de Tocqueville continues, saying ancient tyrannies 'to reach the soul, clumsily struck at the body, and the soul, escaping from such blows, rose gloriously above it'. Instead, modern 'democratic' tyranny 'leaves the body alone and goes straight for the soul' (de Tocqueville 1969: 255). This step from chains and hangmen to individual manipulation and control of ideology and behaviour has been christened by Foucault the transition from the disciplinary society to the society of control. But, as we know, to name something is completely different from discovering it. In this case, the creature had already been discovered and had a name. What Foucault with his renowned ability did was to give it a new, and very attractive, name, different from the one everybody knew. Nevertheless, it cannot be said that we are in the presence of a fundamental theoretical innovation.

The first part of the book concludes with a chapter devoted to alternatives within the empire. It begins with a statement as perplexing as it is radical: 'The multitude called the Empire into being' (p. 43). Contrary to most common interpretations within the left, Hardt and Negri believe that the empire is not the creation of a world capitalist coalition under the American bourgeois hegemony but the (defensive?) response of capital to the class struggles against contemporary forms of domination and oppression nurtured by 'the multitude's desire for liberation' (ibid.). At this point, Hardt and Negri enter a terrain plagued with contradictions. They insist that the empire is good since it represents a 'step forward' in overcoming colonialism and imperialism. They insist on this even after assuring us, with the help of Hegel, that the fact that the empire 'is good in itself' does not mean that it is good 'for itself' (p. 42). They continue: 'We claim that Empire is better in the same way that Marx insists that capitalism is better than the forms of society and modes of production that came before it' (p. 43). However, a few lines earlier, the authors say that the empire 'constructs its own relationships of power based on exploitation that are in many respects more brutal than those it destroyed' (ibid.). Despite this, the empire is 'better' because, they assert, it enhances the potential for liberation of the multitude, an assumption that has not been confirmed by experience and that, in Hardt and Negri's case, is surrounded by a dense metaphysical and, in certain ways, religious halo, as I shall show in the final pages of this work. Where that blissful liberating potential is and how such possibilities could be realized is something the authors explain, in a simplistic and unsatisfactory way, in the last chapter of their book.

On the other hand, to say that the empire is 'better' means that the real capitalist world order – and this is precisely the empire – is something different from capitalism. Marx's argument referred to two different modes of production and compared the possibilities and perspectives opened by capitalism to the ones offered by the decay of feudalism. Are the authors trying to say that the empire means the overcoming of capitalism? Is it that we have transcended it without anybody noticing such a fabulous historical change? Are we now in a new and better society with renewed possibilities for liberating and emancipating practices?

It seems that Hardt and Negri have built a straw man, an irrational and immutable leftist who, in the face of the challenges posed by globalization, insists on opposing local resistance to a process that is global by nature. Local means, in most cases, 'national', but this distinction is irrelevant in their analysis. They say that the strategy of local resistance 'misidentifies and thus masks the enemy' (p. 45). Since Hardt and Negri want to talk politics seriously – and without this being a formal concession to Schmitt but to Clausewitz, Lenin and Mao – who is the enemy then? The answer to this very concrete question could not be more disappointing since we are told that 'The enemy is not a subject but, rather, is a specific regime of global relations that we call Empire' (pp. 45–6). National struggles conceal the view of the real mechanisms of empire, of the existing alternatives, and of the liberating potentials that agitate in its womb. Hence, the oppressed and exploited masses of the world are convened for a final battle against a regime of global relations. The beloved Don Quixote appears once again, after several centuries, to tilt at new

31

windmills while the sordid millers, ignoring the multitude's rage, continue with business as usual, ruling their countries, exploiting the masses and manipulating the culture.

Hardt and Negri view the empire as the historic overcoming of modernity, a period for which they supply a somewhat distorted vision. Indeed, modernity left a legacy of 'fratricidal wars, devastating "development," cruel "civilization," and previously unimagined violence' (p. 46). The scenario that modernity presents is one of tragedy, signified by the presence of 'Concentration camps, nuclear weapons, genocidal wars, slavery, apartheid' (ibid.). And from modernity, Hardt and Negri deduce a straight line that leads to the nation-state without mediation. The nation-state is nothing but the 'ineluctable condition for imperialist domination and innumerable wars'. And if now such an aberration 'is disappearing from the world scene, then good riddance!' (ibid.).

There are several problems with this peculiar interpretation of modernity. In the first place, it is a mistake to offer an extremely unilateral and biased reading of it. Hardt and Negri are right when they enumerate some of the horrors produced by modernity (or perhaps *in* modernity and not necessarily because of it), but while doing so they forget some other results of modernity, such as the flowering of individual liberties; the relative equality established in the economic, political and social terrains, at least in the developed capitalisms; universal suffrage and mass democracy; the coming of socialism despite the frustration generated by some of its concrete experiences, such as the Soviet Union; secularization and the lay state that emancipated the masses from the tyranny of tradition and religion; rationality and the scientific spirit; popular education; economic progress; and many other accomplishments. These too are part of modernity's inheritance, and many of these accomplishments were achieved thanks to popular struggles and in strenuous opposition to the bourgeoisie. Second, do Hardt and Negri really believe that before modernity none of the social evils and human aberrations that plagued the modern world was already there? Do they by any chance believe that the world was inhabited by Rousseau's noble savages? Do they not situate themselves in the same position as the critics of Niccolò Machiavelli who denounced the Florentine theoretician for being the 'inventor' of political crimes, treason and fraud? Have they not heard about the Punic or Peloponnesian wars, the destruction of Carthage, the sack of Rome and, more recently, the conquest and occupation of the American continent? Do they believe that before modernity there were no genocides, apartheid or slavery? As Marx did well to remind us, we are victims of both the development of capitalism and its lack of development.

Once Hardt and Negri have asserted the substantive and historical continuity between modernity and the nation-state, they rush to reject the antiquated 'proletarian internationalism' because it presupposes an acknowledgement of the nation-state and its crucial role as an agent of capitalist exploitation. Given the ineluctable decadence of the nation-state's powers and the global nature of capitalism, this type of internationalism is both anachronistic and technically reactionary. But this is not all: together with the 'proletarian internationalism', the idea of the existence of an 'international cycle of struggles' disappears. The new battles, whose paradigmatic examples are the Tiananmen Square revolt, the Palestinian Intifada, the 1992 race riots in Los Angeles and the South Korean strikes of 1996, are specific and motivated by 'immediate regional concerns in such a way that they could in no respect be linked together as a globally expanding chain of revolt. None of these events inspired a cycle of struggles, because the desires and needs they expressed could not be translated into different contexts' (p. 54).

From this categorical assertion, for which it would require considerable effort to provide supporting evidence, our authors announce a new paradox: 'in our much celebrated age of communication, *struggles have become all but incommunicable*' (p. 54, emphasis in original). The reasons for this incommunicability remain shadowy, but we should not lose hope in the face of the impossibility of horizontal communication among the rebels because, in reality, it is a blessing. Under the logic of the empire, Hardt and Negri tell their impatient readers, the message of these battles will travel vertically on a global scale, attacking the imperial constitution in its nucleus – or, what they call with a meaningful slip, jumping vertically 'to the virtual center of Empire' (p. 58).

Here, new and more formidable problems besiege their argument. In the first place, those that derive from the very dangerous confusion between axiomatic assumptions and empirical observations. To say that the popular battles are incommunicable is an extremely important assertion. Unfortunately, Hardt and Negri do not offer any evidence to demonstrate whether this is mere supposition or the result of a historical or empirical investigation. Faced with this silence, there are abundant reasons for suspecting that this *problematique* reflects the less than healthy influence of Niklas Luhmann and Jürgen Habermas over Hardt and Negri. A quick exploration of the nebulous concepts put forward by these German scholars is enough to confirm the scant utility that their constructions have when it comes to analysing popular struggles. This, though, does not prevent either of them from being extremely popular among the ranks of the disoriented Italian left. In this sense, the Luhmannian theses on social incommensurability and Habermas's proposals concerning communicative action seem to have greatly influenced Hardt and Negri, at least to a greater extent than they are willing to recognize. But leaving aside this brief *excursus* towards the sociology of knowledge, if the incommunicability of the struggles prevents them from inflaming the desires and needs of people from other countries, how can we explain the speed with which the erroneously named 'anti-globalization' movement spread all over the world? Do Hardt and Negri really believe that the events in Chiapas, Paris and Seoul were truly incommunicable? How can they ignore the fact that the Zapatistas, and especially sub-commander Marcos, became international icons for the neoliberal globalization critics and for the anti-capitalist battles in five continents, influencing important developments in these conflicts waged at local and national levels?

Second, Hardt and Negri maintain that one of the main obstacles preventing the communicability of the battles is the 'absence of a recognition of a common enemy against which the struggles are directed' (p. 56). We do not know whether or not this was the case among the French or South Korean strikers, but we suspect that they had a clearer idea than our authors regarding the identity of their antagonists. Concerning the Zapatistas' experience, Hardt and Negri's thesis is completely wrong. From the beginning of their battle, the Chiapanecos had no doubts and knew perfectly well who their enemies were. Aware of this reality, they organized an extraordinary event in the depths of the Lacandona jungle – an international conference against neoliberal globalization, attended by hundreds of participants from around the world who discussed some of today's most burning problems. The ability of the Zapatistas to convoke a conference of this type refutes, in practice, another of Hardt and Negri's theses – the one that bemoans the lack of a suitable common and cosmopolitan language into which to translate the languages used in diverse national struggles (p. 57). The successive conferences that took place in the Lacandona jungle, together with the demonstrations against neoliberal globalization and the world social forums held in Porto Alegre, Brazil, show that, contrary to what is said in *Empire*, there is a common language and a common understanding among the different social forces fighting the dictatorship of capital.

If the old battles are no longer relevant – Marx's old mole has died, to be replaced by the 'infinite undulations' of the modern snake, according to Hardt and Negri – the strategy of the anti-capitalist journeys has to change. National conflicts are not communicated horizontally but jump directly to the virtual centre of the empire, and the old 'weak links' of the imperialist chain have disappeared. The articulations of the global power that exhibited a particular vulnerability before the action of insurgent forces no longer exist. Therefore, 'To achieve significance, every struggle must attack at the heart of the Empire, at its strength' (p. 58). Surprisingly, after having argued in the book's Preface that the empire 'is a decentered and deterritorializing apparatus of rule' (p. xii), the reader stumbles across the novelty that local and national battles must rise at the centre of the empire, though our authors rush to explain that they are not referring to a territorial centre but to a (supposedly) virtual one. Given that the empire includes all the components of the social orders, even the deeper ones, and knowing that it has no limits or frontiers, the notions of 'outside' and 'inside' have lost their meaning. Now everything is inside the empire, and its nucleus, its heart, can be attacked from anywhere. If we are to believe Hardt and Negri, the Zapatista uprising in Chiapas, the invasion of land by the Landless Workers' Movement in Brazil (MST) or the pot-banging protesters and pickets in Argentina are no different from the 11 September attacks in New York and Washington. Is it indeed like this? Judging from the different types of reactions to all these events, it would seem that this is not the perception held by those at the 'Empire's heart'. On the other hand, what meaning should we assign to this expression? Are we talking of the capitalist nucleus, the centre, the imperialist coalition with its widening net of concentric circles revolving round American capitalist power, or what? Who are the concrete subjects at the 'Empire's heart'? Where are they? What is their articulation with the processes of production and circulation of the international capitalist economy? Which institutions normatively and ideologically crystallize their domination? Who are their political representatives? Or is it just a set of immaterial rules and procedures? The book not only does not offer any answers to these questions, but does not even formulate the questions.

At this stage, Hardt and Negri's theorization makes its way to a real disaster. By asserting that everything is inside the empire, their theory completely removes from our horizon of visibility the fact that structural hierarchies and asymmetries exist precisely there, and that such differences do not disappear simply because someone has declared that everything is inside the empire and nothing is left outside. Studies undertaken by Latin American scholars and writers over decades do agree, beyond the differences, on the fact that the categories of 'centre' and 'periphery' enjoy a certain capacity, at least at first, to produce a more refined portrait of the international system. Everything seems to indicate that such a distinction is more useful than ever in the current circumstances, because, among other things, the growing economic marginalization of the South has sharply accentuated pre-existing asymmetries. In order to confirm this assertion it is enough to remind ourselves of what the United Nations Development Programme's (UNDP) annual reports point out with regard to human development: if at the beginning of the 1960s the ratio between the richest 20 per cent and the poorest 20 per cent of the world population was 30 to 1, at the end of the twentieth century this ratio had grown to almost 75 to 1. It is true that Bangladesh and Haiti are inside the empire, but are they because of this in a position comparable to that of the United States, France, Germany or Japan? Hardt and Negri claim that even though they are not identical from the production and circulation point of view, between 'the United States and Brazil, Britain and India [...] are no differences of nature, only differences of degree' (p. 335).

This categorical conclusion cancels the last forty years of debates and research that took place not only in Latin America but also in the rest of the Third World, and it brings us back to the American theories in vogue in the 1950s and at the beginning of the 1960s, when authors such as Walter W. Rostow, Bert Hoselitz and many others elaborated their ahistorical models of economic development. According to these constructions, in both nineteenth-century Europe and the United States and in the historical processes that took place in the middle of the twentieth century in Latin America, Asia and Africa, economic growth followed a linear and evolutionist path, beginning in underdevelopment and concluding in development. This type of reasoning was based on two false assumptions: first, that societies located at either extreme of the continuum share the same nature and that they are essentially the same. Their differences, when existent, were only in terms of degree, as Hardt and Negri would later say, an assertion that was, and still is, completely false. The second assumption: the organization of international markets has no structural asymmetries that could affect the chances of development for nations in the periphery. For those authors mentioned above, terms such as 'dependency' or 'imperialism' were not useful when describing the realities of the system and they were more than anything else a tribute to political – and hence not scientific – approaches, with which an understanding of economic development was sought. The so-called 'obstacles' for development lacked structural foundations. Instead they were the product of clumsy political decisions, unfortunate and poorly informed choices made by the rulers, or easily removable inertial factors. In Hardt and Negri's terms, all the countries were 'inside' the system.

In this imaginary return to the past, it is important to remember the following: at the beginning of the 1970s, the Latin American debate about dependency, imperialism and neo-colonialism had reached its apogee, and its resonance deafened the Academy and American political circles. Its impact was of such magnitude that Henry Kissinger, then chief of the National Security Council and on his way to becoming Secretary of State under Richard Nixon, considered it necessary to intervene on more than one occasion in the discussions and debates caused by the Latin Americans. Hardt and Negri's thesis about the non-differentiation of the nations within the empire calls to mind the cynical comments made by Kissinger about this topic. Expressing his rejection of the idea of Third World economic dependency and questioning the extension and importance of the structural asymmetries in the world economy, Kissinger observed: 'today we are all dependent. We live in an interdependent world. The United States depend on the Honduran bananas as much as Honduras depends on the American computers.'[2] As can be easily concluded, some of the statements expressed with such finality in *Empire* – for instance, that there are no more differences between the centre and the periphery of the system, that there is no longer an 'outside', that the players merely differ in degree, etc. – are far from new. These affirmations began to circulate through the words of theoreticians clearly affiliated to the right, who opposed a theory of 'interdependence' and imperialism, and who refused to accept that the international economy was characterized by the radical asymmetry that separated the nations in the centre of the system from those at the periphery.

Hardt and Negri conclude this section of the book by introducing the two-headed eagle, the emblem of the old Austro-Hungarian Empire, as a convenient symbol for the current empire. However, it is necessary to introduce a little reworking of this image since the two heads would have to look inwards, as if they were about to attack each other. The first head of the imperial eagle represents the juridical structure – not the economic foundations – of the empire. As we have said, there is very little political economy in this book and the absence of the most elementary mention of the economic structure of the empire in what is outlined as its emblematic image reveals the strange paths through which our authors have ventured and on which they have

---

2. Henry Kissinger is considered by the novelist and playwright Gore Vidal to be 'the most conspicuous criminal of war loose around the world' (cf. Saxe-Fernández et al. 2001: 25).

completely lost their way. That is why the eagle's second head, staring at the one that represents the empire's juridical order, symbolizes 'the plural multitude of productive, creative subjectivities of globalization' (p. 60). This multitude is the true

> absolutely positive force that pushes the dominating power toward an abstract and empty unification, to which it appears as the distinct alternative. From this perspective, when the constituted power of Empire appears merely as privation of being and production, as a simple abstract and empty trace of the constituent power of the multitude, then we will be able to recognize the real standpoint of our analysis. (pp. 62–3)

In short: those interested in exploring the alternatives to the empire will find very little help in this section of the book. What they will find is a death certificate for the archaic 'proletarian internationalism' (without any mention of the new internationalism that erupted strongly from Seattle);[3] a petition of principles in the sense that the popular struggles are incommunicable and lack a common language; an embarrassing silence regarding the relationship with a concrete enemy whom the omnipotent multitude faces or, in the best case, an immobilizing vagueness ('a regime of global relationships'); the disappearance of the 'weaker links' and the distinction between centre and periphery; and that the old distinction between strategy and tactics has disappeared because now there is only one way of battling against the empire and it is strategic and tactical at the same time. This way is the rising of a constituent counter-power that emerges from its womb, something hard to understand in light of Hardt and Negri's rejection of dialectics. The only lesson that can be learnt is

3. For more on this, I suggest looking at the compilation prepared by the Observatorio Social de América Latina of CLACSO in an issue devoted to the 'new internationalism' with texts by Noam Chomsky, Ana Esther Ceceña, Christophe Aguiton, Rafael Freire, Walden Bello, Jaime Estay and Francisco Pineda (OSAL, 6, January 2002).

that we must trust that the multitude will finally assume the tasks assigned them by Hardt and Negri. How and when this will occur cannot be found in the book's contents. There is no discussion about the ways of fighting; the organizational models (assuming, as the authors do, that the parties and labour unions are illustrious corpses); the mobilization strategies and the confrontational tactics; the articulation among the economic, political and ideological conflicts and oppositions; the long-term objectives and revolutionary agenda; the political instruments used to put an end to the iniquities of global capitalism; international alliances; the military aspects of subversion promoted by the multitude; and many other topics of similar transcendence. Neither is there any attempt to relate the current postmodern discussion about the subversive impulse of the multitudes to previous debates about the labour movement and anti-capitalist forces in general, as if the phase in which we are now had not emerged from the unfolding of past social struggles but had erupted, instead, from the philosophers' heads.

What we do find in this part of the book is a vague exhortation to trust in the transformational potential of the multitude, who, in a mysterious and unpredictable way, will some day overcome all resistance and blocks, and subdue its enemies to ... To do what? To build what type of society? Its intellectual mentors still do not say.

3 Markets, transnational corporations and national economies

A Recurrent Confusion

Hard and Negri's naive acceptance of a crucial aspect of world market ideology clearly illustrates the consequences of their radical incomprehension of contemporary capitalism. Inexplicably stubborn in maintaining the not very innocent myth that nation-states are close to disappearing completely, the authors make their own, as if it were a truth revealed by a prophet, the opinion of the former US Secretary of Labor, Robert Reich, who wrote:

> as almost every factor of production – money, technology, factories, and equipment – moves effortlessly across borders, the very idea of a [national] economy is becoming meaningless. In the future 'there will be no *national* products or technologies, no national corporations, no national industries. There will no longer be national economies, at least as we have come to understand that concept.' (p. 151)

It is hard to believe that an intellectual of Toni Negri's calibre, who in the past has shown a strong interest in the study of economics, could cite an opinion such as the one above. First of all, Reich shrewdly speaks of 'almost every factor of production', an elegant way of avoiding the embarrassing fact that there is another crucial factor of production, the labour force, which does not 'move effortlessly across borders'. This belief in the free mobility of productive factors is to be found at the heart of corporate American ideology, determined as it is to embellish the assumed virtues of the free market at the same time as it condemns any type of state intervention that does not favour monopolies or oligopolies or that introduces at least a minimum level of popular or democratic control over economic processes. From their stratospheric platform, Hardt and Negri seem to ignore the fact that Reich was the Secretary of Labor in a government that presided over one of the most dramatic periods of wealth and income concentration in the history of the United States. It was a time when waged labour saw some of the most important pieces of labour legislation dismantled and when precariousness reached unprecedented levels not only in the rural districts of Alabama and California but also in the Upper West Side of Manhattan, where hundreds of elegant stores recruited illegal immigrants to assist their clients, paying them salaries well below the legal minimum. Perhaps the authors refused to acknowledge that none of these workers would have crossed American borders without considerable effort. The history of these migrants is one of violence and death, pain and misery, suffering and humiliation. And it is a history in which the crucial player is the nation-state that Hardt and Negri describe as 'declining'. Before writing about such issues, it would have been appropriate had the authors interviewed an undocumented worker from Mexico, El Salvador or Haiti to ask him what the expression '*la migra*' means, a term used to refer to the United States' immigration police, the very mention of which terrifies the immigrants. Or maybe the authors could have asked how much the worker had to pay to enter the United States illegally, how many of his friends died in the attempt and what the word 'coyote' means on the Californian border. Have they not heard about the unsuccessful migrants who died in the desert under a baking sun (but comforted by Reich's words)? Can they ignore the fact that every year the Mexican–American frontier takes more human lives than the infamous Berlin Wall throughout its entire existence? It would also be appropriate to ask similar questions of illegal immigrants in France and the rest of Europe. A quick look at UNDP or the International Labor Organization (ILO) reports would have saved them from making major mistakes such as as the one mentioned above.

It is not their only mistake. Our authors seem to believe that money, technology, factories and equipment are also subject to unlimited mobility. Money is, no doubt, the most mobile of the four, but even so it is tied to certain restrictions, albeit not extremely strict ones. But what about technology and the rest? Do they really believe that technology and the other factors of production circulate as freely across borders as Reich proclaims? Which technology anyway? Do they mean last generation technology? This is something that even a primary school child already knows. Obviously, technology and its products circulate, but the ones that move more freely are surely not the latest or the best. Third World countries know that they can have access without problems to obsolete or semi-obsolete technologies, relics already abandoned by the nations at the forefront of the planet's technological development. If the best technologies circulate freely as corporate-speak assures us, why is it that we witness so many cases of industrial espionage in all the developed countries? How can we explain industrial piracy, illegal copying and imitations of all types of technologies and products?

That Hardt and Negri accept some of the central assumptions of the ideologues of globalization is a matter of extreme concern. Their belief in the disappearance of national products, companies and industries is absolutely indefensible in the light of daily evidence that shows the vitality, especially in developed countries, of customs taxes, non-tariff barriers and special subsidies through which governments seek to favour their national products, companies and economic activities. The authors live in countries where protectionism has an extraordinary strength and can be ignored only by those who insist on denying its existence simply because it has no place in their theory. The American government protects its inhabitants from foreign competition from Mexican strawberries, Brazilian cars, Argentine seamless steel pipes, Salvadorian textiles, Chilean grapes and Uruguayan meat, while on the other side of the Atlantic, the European citizens are safely protected by 'Fortress Europe' which, while hypocritically proclaiming the virtues of free trade, seals its doors against the 'threat' posed by the vibrant economies of Africa, Latin America and Asia.

Regarding the declared disappearance of national companies, a simple test would be enough to demonstrate this mistake. For example, Hardt and Negri should try to convince a friendly government to expropriate a local branch of a 'global' firm (and, therefore, supposedly unattached to any national base) such as Microsoft, McDonald's or Ford; or, if they prefer, they could try to do this with Deutsche Bank, Siemens, Shell or Unilever. Then we would have only to wait and see who would step forward to demand that the decision be revoked. If the companies were truly global, it would be the job of Kofi Annan, or of the general director of the World Trade Organization (WTO), to appear in front of the government involved in order to put pressure on it in the name of global markets and the world economy. However, it is more likely that, instead of those characters, an ambassador from the United States, Germany or the United Kingdom would turn up to demand, with their usual rudeness and insolence, the immediate reversal of the decision under the threat of punishing the country with all types of sanctions and penalties. If this hypothetical example seems too complicated, Hardt and Negri should ask themselves, for example, who was the Boeing representative in the tough negotiations with European Union officials for the commercial competition with Airbus. Do they believe that the interests of the former were defended by a CEO from Bangladesh who had received his MBA from the University of Chicago or instead by top American government officials with the help of their ambassador in Brussels and acting together with the White House? In the real world, and not in the nebulous republic imagined by philosophers, the latter is what really occurs. This is something that any student of economics learns only two weeks into classes.

Can Hardt and Negri ignore the fact that the 200 mega-corporations that prevail in the world markets register a combined total of sales that is greater than the GNP of all the countries in the world combined except for the nine largest? Their total annual income reaches the $7,100 trillion threshold and they are as big as the combined wealth of 80 per cent of the world population, whose income barely reaches $3,900 trillion. Despite this, these Leviathans of the world economy employ less than one-third of 1 per cent of the world population (Barlow 1998). The neoliberal globalization ideologists' rhetoric is not enough to disguise the fact that 96 per cent of those 200 global and transnational companies have their headquarters in only eight countries, are legally registered as incorporated companies of eight countries; and their board of directors sit in eight countries of metropolitan capitalism. Less than 2 per cent of their board of directors' members are non-nationals, while more than 85 per cent of all their technological developments have originated within their 'national frontiers'. Their reach is global, but their property and their owners have a clear national base. Their earnings flow from all over the world to their headquarters and the loans necessary to finance their operations are conveniently obtained by their headquarters in the national banks at interest rates impossible to find in peripheral capitalisms, thanks to which they can easily displace their competitors (Boron et al 1999: 233; Boron 2000b: 117–23).

Noam Chomsky, for instance, cites a study by Winfried Ruigrock and Rob Van Tulder on the top 100 corporations of the 1993 *Fortune* list according to which 'virtually all of the world's largest corporations have experienced a decisive support from government policies and trade barriers to make them viable.' In addition, these authors also noted that at least 20 companies would not have survived by themselves have their governments not 'intervened by either socialising losses or by simple takeovers when the companies were in trouble' (Chomsky 1998, Kapstein

1991/92, Ruigrock and Van Tulder 1995). In short, despite what the authors of *Empire* assert, nation-states still are crucial players in the world economy, and national economies still exist.

The postmodern logic of global capital

In line with the argument developed in the previous section, Hardt and Negri state that a profound change in the logic with which global capital operates has taken place with the constitution of the empire. The predominant logic these days is that of postmodernism, with its emphasis on exalting the instantaneous, the always changing profiles of desires, the cult of individual election, the 'perpetual shopping and the consumption of commodities and commodified images [...] difference and multiplicity [...] fetishism and simulacra, its continued fascination with the new and with fashion' (p. 152). All these lead our authors to conclude that marketing strategies follow a postmodern logic, since marketing is a corporate practice intended to maximize sales from the commercial recognition and exploitation of differences. As populations become increasingly hybrid, the possibility for creating new 'target markets' is enhanced. The consequence is that marketing unfolds an endless array of commercial strategies: 'one for gay Latino males between the ages of eighteen and twenty-two, another for Chinese-American teenage girls, and so forth' (p. 152).

Aware that, by pretending to infer the global logic of capital from marketing strategies, they are on a slippery slope, Hardt and Negri take a step forwards to assure us that the same postmodern logic also prevails at the heart of the capitalist economy: the sphere of production. For this, they recall some recent developments in the management field, where it is stated that corporations must be 'mobile, flexible, and able to deal with difference' (p. 153). As could have been foreseen, the naive acceptance of these assumed advances of 'management science' – in truth, strategies to strengthen the extraction of surplus value – led Hardt and Negri to a completely idealized vision of contemporary global corporations. These appear as 'much more diverse and fluid culturally than the parochial modern corporations of previous years'. A consequence of this greater diversity and fluidity is evident in the fact that, according to the authors, 'the old modernist forms of racist and sexist theory are the explicit enemies of this new corporate culture' (p. 153). Because of this, global companies are anxious to include:

> difference within their realm and thus aim to maximize creativity, free play, and diversity in the corporate workplace. People of all different races, sexes, and sexual orientations should potentially be included in the corporation; the daily routine of the workplace should be rejuvenated with unexpected changes and an atmosphere of fun. Break down the old boundaries and let one hundred flowers bloom! (p. 153)

After reading these lines, we cannot avoid asking to what extent corporations are home to the relationships of production; are the salaried exploited or, in contrast, are they real earthly paradises? It does not seem to require a management expert to conclude that the rosy description given by the authors bears little relationship to reality, since sexism, racism and homophobia are practices that still enjoy enviable health in the postmodern global corporation. Maybe this improved corporate atmosphere has something to do with the fact that, as reported in the *New England Journal of Medicine*, during the apogee of American prosperity, 'African-American men in Harlem had less probabilities of reaching the age of 65 than men in Bangladesh' (Chomsky 1993: 278). Hardt and Negri constantly fall against the subtle ropes of corporate literature and the free market ideologists. If we were to accept their points of view – actually the points of view of the business school gurus – the whole debate around the despotism of capital within the corporation loses its meaning, as it does every time more demands in favour of the democratization of firms are made by theoreticians of Robert A. Dahl's stature (Dahl 1995: 134–5). Apparently, the structural tyranny of capital vanishes when wage-labourers go to work not to earn a living but to entertain themselves in an agreeable climate that allows them to express their desires without restriction. This portrait hardly squares with the stories reported even by the most capital-involved sectors of the press about the extension of the work day in the global corporation, the devastating impact of labour flexibility, the degradation of work and of the workplace, the growing frequency with which people are laid off, the precariousness of employment, the trend towards an aggressive concentration of salaries within the company, not to mention horror stories such as the exploitation of children by many global corporations.

It seems unnecessary to insist, before these two authors who identify themselves as communists and scholars of Marx, on the fact that the logic of capital, be it global or national, has little to do with the image projected by business school theoreticians or eclectic postmodern philosophers. Capital moves through an inexorable logic of profit-generation, whatever the social or environmental costs may be. In order to maximize profits and increase security in the long term, capital travels all over the world and is capable of establishing itself anywhere. The political conditions are a matter of major importance, especially if there is a need to maintain an obedient and well-behaved labour force. Corporate blackmail is also extremely relevant, given that the global firms, with 'their' government's support, seek to gain benefits from the extraordinary concessions made by the hungry states of the impoverished periphery. These concessions range from generous tax exemptions of all kinds to the implementation of labour legislation contrary to workers' interests, or of the type that discourages or weakens the activism of labour unions capable of disturbing the normal atmosphere of business. In the developed world, instead, it is more difficult to dismantle workers' advances and achievements, and the pro-labour legislation sanctioned in the golden period of the Keynesian state, but this is compensated for by the greater size of the markets in societies where social progress has created a pattern of mass consumption not usually available in the peripheral countries.

Transnational corporations and the nation-state

Chapter 3.5 of Hardt and Negri's book is devoted to the mixed constitution of the empire. It opens, however, with a surprising epigraph that demonstrates the unusual penetration of bourgeois prejudices even into the minds of two intellectuals as lucid and cultured as Hardt and Negri. The epigraph is a statement made not by a great philosopher or a distinguished economist, nor by a renowned statesman or a popular leader. It is, instead, a few words pronounced by Bill Gates: 'One of the wonderful things about the information highway is that virtual equity is far easier to achieve than real-world equity ... We are all created equal in the virtual world' (p. 304).

Two brief comments. First, it is hard to understand the reason why a chapter devoted to examining the problems of the mixed constitution of the empire begins with a banal quote from Bill Gates about the supposed equity of the information highway. Maybe it is because quoting Gates has become fashionable among some European and American progressive intellectuals. The reader, even one who is well disposed, cannot but feel irritation before this tribute paid to the richest man in the world, someone who is the most genuine personification of a world order that, supposedly, Hardt and Negri fervently desire to change.

Second, and even more important, Gates is wrong, deeply wrong. Not all of us have been created equal in the information world and the fantastic virtual universe. Surely, Gates has never been in contact with even one of the three billion people in the world who have never made or received a phone call. Gates and Hardt and Negri should remember that in very poor countries, such as Afghanistan for instance, only five out of a thousand people have access to a telephone. This horrifying figure is far from being exclusive to Afghanistan. In many areas in southern Asia, in sub-Saharan Africa, and in some underdeveloped countries in Latin America and the Caribbean, the figures are not much better (Wresch 1996). For most of the world's population, Gates's comments are a joke, if not an insult to their miserable and inhumane living conditions.

Leaving aside this unfortunate beginning, the chapter introduces a division of capitalist development into three stages. The first extends throughout the eighteenth and nineteenth centuries. It is a period of competitive capitalism, characterized according to Hardt and Negri by 'relatively little need of state intervention at home and abroad' (p. 305). For the authors, the protectionist policies of the UK, the USA, France, Belgium, Holland and Germany, and the policies of colonial expansion promoted and implemented by the respective national governments, do not qualify as 'state intervention'. In the same manner, the legislation passed, with different degrees of thoroughness in all these countries over a long period and destined to repress the workers, would also not qualify as examples of state intervention in economic and social life. It should be taken into consideration that such legislation includes the Anti-Combination Acts of England, the Le Chappellier law in France, the anti-socialist legislation of Chancellor Bismarck in Germany, who condemned thousands of workers to exile, and the legal norms that made possible the brutal repression of workers in the United States, symbolized by the massacre of Haymarket Square, Chicago, on 1 May 1886. Gramsci formulated some very precise observations about the 'Southern Question' in which he demonstrated that the complex system of alliances that made Italian unification possible overlay a set of sophisticated economic policies that in fact supported the dominant coalition. It was Gramsci who pointed out the 'theoretical mistake' of the liberal doctrines that celebrated the supposedly hands-off attitude, the passivity of the state in relation

51

to the capitalist accumulation process. In his *Quaderni*, Gramsci wrote: 'The *laissez-faire* is also a mode of state regulation, introduced and maintained by legislative and constraining means. It is a deliberate policy, aware of its own objectives, and not the spontaneous and automatic expression of the economic events. Consequently, the *laissez-faire* liberalism is a political program' (Gramsci 1971: 160).

The reason for this gross error must be found in the inability of liberal writers to recognize the fact that the distinction between the political society and the civil society, between economics and politics, 'is made and presented as if it were an organic distinction, when it is merely a methodological distinction' (ibid.). The 'passivity' of the state when the fox enters the henhouse cannot be conceived as the inaction proper to a neutral player. This behaviour is called complicity or, in some cases, conspiracy. These brief examples are enough to prove that conventional knowledge is not capable of providing adequate guidelines to explain some of the central features of the first period identified by Hardt and Negri. Certainly, the passivity of the state was not one of them. It is true that, in comparison with what happened in the period following the great depression, the levels of state intervention were lower. But this does not mean that there was no intervention, or that the need for it was weaker. On the contrary, there was a great need for state intervention and the different bourgeois governments responded adequately to this need. Naturally, after the First World War and the 1929 crisis, these needs increased to an extraordinary degree, but that should not lead us to believe that before these dates the state did not play a primary role in the process of capitalist accumulation.

The most serious problem with Hardt and Negri's interpretation emerges when they get to the 'third stage' in the history of the marriage between the state and capital. In their own words: 'Today a third phase of this relationship has fully matured, in which large transnational corporations have effectively surpassed the jurisdiction and authority of nation-states. It would seem, then, that this centuries-long dialectic has come to an end: the state has been defeated and corporations now rule the earth!' (p. 306, emphasis in original).

This statement is not only wrong but also exposes the authors to new rebuffs. Worried about having gone too far with their anti-state enthusiasm, they warn us that it is necessary 'to take a much more nuanced look at how the relationship between state and capital has changed' (p. 307). It is at the very least perplexing that, after having written this sentence, the authors did not proceed with the same conviction to erase the previous sentence. This confirms the suspicion that the first one represents adequately enough what they think about the subject. For them, one of the crucial features of the current period is the displacement of state functions and political tasks into other social life levels and domains. Reversing the historical process by which the nation-state 'expropriated' the political and administrative functions retained until then by the aristocracy and local magnates, such tasks and functions have been re-appropriated by somebody else in this third stage in the history of capital. But by whom? We do not know, because in Hardt and Negri's argument there is a meaningful silence at this point. Hardt and Negri begin assuring us in an axiomatic way that the concept of national sovereignty is losing its effectiveness, without bothering to provide some type of empirical reference to support this thesis. The same happens with the famous thesis about 'the autonomy of the political'. If evidence for the first thesis is completely absent, all that can be said is that it is a commonplace of contemporary bourgeois ideology; concerning the second thesis, Hardt and Negri are completely wrong. To support their interpretation, they maintain: 'Today a notion of politics as an independent sphere of the determination of consensus and a sphere of mediation among conflicting social forces has very little room to exist' (p. 307). Question: when and where was politics that 'independent sphere' or that simple 'sphere of mediation'? To this it could be answered that what is in crisis is not so much politics – which might well be in crisis, but for other reasons – but a Schmittian conception of politics, which progressive European and American intellectuals cultivated with an obsessive passion for many years. As a result of that addiction, the confusing doctrinal constructions of Nazi theoretician Carl Schmitt – not only an academic but also a leading judge in the Third Reich – were interpreted as a great contribution to political theory capable of providing an escape route for the oft-proclaimed 'crisis of Marxism'. But, contrary to Schmitt's teachings, politics in capitalist societies was never an autonomous sphere. This discussion is so well known, generating rivers of ink in the 1960s and 1980s, that there is no need to summarize it now. For the purpose of this book, a brief reference to a couple of works that approach this problem in a direct manner (Meiskins Wood 1995: 19–48; Boron 1997: 95–137) will suffice. In any case, our authors are closer to the truth when they write, a few lines later: 'Politics does not disappear; what disappears is any notion of the autonomy of the political' (p. 307). Once again, the problem here is less with politics – which has undoubtedly changed – than with the absurd notion of the autonomy of politics and of the political, nurtured for decades by angry anti-Marxist academics and intellectuals, who desire to maintain, against all the evidence, a fragmentary vision of the social, typical of what Gyorg Lukács characterized as bourgeois thought (Lukács 1971).

In Hardt and Negri's interpretation, the decline experienced by the autonomy of politics gave place to an ultra-economicist conception of the consensus, 'determined more significantly by economic factors, such as the equilibria of the trade balances and speculation on the value of currencies' (p. 307). In this way, the Gramscian theorization that saw the consensus as the capacity of the dominant alliance to guarantee an intellectual and moral direction that would establish it as the avant-garde of the development of national energies, is entirely left out of the authors' analysis of the state in its current stage. Instead, the consensus appears as the mechanical reflection of the economic news, a set of mercantile calculation with no room left for political mediations lost in the darkness of time. Its reductionism and economicism completely distort the complexity of the consensus construction process in contemporary capitalism, and, in addition, they do not fail to pass the test that demonstrates how on innumerable occasions significant political turbulence occurred at moments in which the economic variables were moving in the 'right direction', as European and American history of the 1960s demonstrates. Besides, times of deep economic crisis did not necessarily translate into the swift collapse of pre-existing political consensuses. Popular passivity and acquiescence were noticeable, for example, in the ominous decade of the 1930s in France and Britain, something very different from what was occurring in neighbouring Germany. In consequence, it is undeniable that, given that politics is not a sphere autonomous from social life, there is an intimate connection between economic factors and political, social, cultural and international factors that, at a certain moment, crystallizes in the construction of a long-lasting political consensus. That is why any reductionist conceptual scheme, either economicist or politicist, is incapable of explaining reality.

The conclusion of the authors' analysis is extraordinarily important and can be summarized in this way: the decline of the political as an autonomous sphere 'signals the decline, too, of any independent space where revolution could emerge in the national political regime, or where social space could be transformed using the instruments of the state' (pp. 307–8). The traditional ideas of building a counter-power or of opposing a national resistance against the state have been losing more and more relevance in the current circumstances. The main functions of the state have migrated to other spheres and domains of the social life, especially towards the 'mechanisms of command on the global level of the transnational corporations' (p. 308). The result of this process was something like the destruction or suicide of the national democratic capitalist state, whose sovereignty fragmented and dispersed among a vast collection of new agencies, groups and organizations such as 'banks, international organisms of planning, and so forth [...] which all increasingly refer for legitimacy to the transnational level of power' (p. 308). In relation to the possibilities opened before this transformation, the verdict of our authors is radical and unappealing: 'the decline of the nation-state is not simply the result of an ideological position that might be reversed by an act of political will: it is a structural and irreversible process' (p. 336). The dispersed fragments of the state's old sovereignty and its inherent capacity to inspire obedience to its mandates, have been recovered and reconverted 'by a whole series of global juridico-economic bodies, such as GATT, the World Trade Organization, the World Bank, and the IMF' (ibid.). Given that the globalization of the production and circulation of goods caused a progressive loss of efficacy and effectiveness in national political and juridical structures which were powerless to control players, processes and mechanisms that greatly exceeded their possibilities and that displayed their games on a foreign board, there is no sense in trying to resurrect the dead nation-state. Aijaz Ahmad (2004: 51) provided a timely reminder that it was none other than Madeleine Albright who, as Secretary of State during the Clinton administration, expounded similar theses by saying that both 'nationality' and 'sovereignty' belonged to an 'outdated repertoire of political theory' unable to account for the 'new structures of globalization and imperatives of "humanitarian intervention"'. The authors assure us that nothing could be more negative for future emancipatory struggles than to fall victim to nostalgia for an old golden era. Still, if it were possible to resurrect the nation-state, there is an even more important reason to give up this enterprise: this institution 'carries with it a whole series of repressive structures and ideologies [...] and any strategy that relies on it should be rejected on that basis' (p. 336). Let us suppose for a moment that we consider this argument valid. In that case we should resign ourselves to contemplating not only the ineluctable decadence of the nation-state but also the fall of the democratic order, a result of centuries of popular struggles that inevitably rest on the state structure. Hardt and Negri do not delve very deeply into this subject of vital importance. Maybe they do not do so because they assume, mistakenly, that it is possible to 'democratize' the markets or a civil society structurally divided into classes. This is not possible, as I have explained carefully elsewhere (Boron 2000b: 73–132). Therefore, which is the way out?

4 Alternative visions of the empire

*The ethical empire, or the postmodern mystification of the
'really existing' empire*

At this stage of their journey, Hardt and Negri have clearly
gone beyond the point of no return, and their analysis of the
'really existing' empire has given place to a poetic and metaphysical construction that, on the one hand, maintains a distant
similarity to reality, and, on the other hand, given precisely those
characteristics, offers scant help to the social forces interested in
transforming the national and international structures of world
capitalism. As Charles Tilly (2003: 26) put it rather bluntly, the
authors 'orbit so far from the concrete realities of contemporary
change that their readers see little but clouds, hazy seas and
nothingness beyond'. The general diagnosis is wrong due to
fatal problems of analysis and interpretation that plague their
theoretical scheme. To this I could add a series of extremely
unfortunate observations and commentaries that a patient reader
could find without great effort. But if the reader were to refute
them, he would be obliged to write a work of extraordinary magnitude. Since that is not my intention, I will continue with my
analysis centred on the weaknesses of the general interpretative
theoretical scheme.

To begin, allow me to reaffirm a very elementary but extremely
important point of departure: it is impossible to do good political
and social philosophy without a solid economic analysis. As I have
shown elsewhere, that was exactly the path chosen by the young
Marx as a political philosopher, once he precociously understood
the limits of a social and political reflection that was not firmly
anchored in a rigorous knowledge of civil society (Boron 2000a).
The science that unveiled the anatomy of civil society and the

most intimate secrets of the new economic organization created by capitalism was political economy. This was the reason why the founder of historical materialism devoted his energies to the new discipline, not to go from one to the other but to anchor his reflections on critiques of the existing social order and his anticipation of a future society in the bedrock of a deep economic analysis. This anchorage in a good political economy, a 'regal way' to reach a thorough knowledge of capitalist society, is precisely what is missing in *Empire*. In fact, the book has very little of economics, and what it has is, in most cases, the conventional version of the economic analysis taught in American or European business schools or the one boosted by the publicists of neo-liberal globalization, combined with some isolated fragments of Marxist political economy. In short: bad economics is used to analyse a topic such as the imperialist system that requires a rigorous treatment of the matter appealing to the best of what political economy could offer. As Michael Rustin persuasively argues, Hardt and Negri's 'description of the major trends of development of both the capitalist economy, and of its major forms of governance, is plainly in accord with much current analysis of glablization' (Rustin 2003: 8).

Consequently, readers will find themselves with a book that attempts to analyse the international order, supposedly an empire, and in which only a couple of times will they stumble across institutions such as the IMF, the World Bank, the WTO and other agencies of the current world order, call it empire or imperialism. For example, the word 'neoliberalism', which refers precisely to the ideology and the economic-political formula prevailing during the last quarter of the twentieth century when the current economic order was rebuilt from head to toe, merely appears throughout the book, in the same way as the Multilateral Agreement on Investments (MAI) and the Washington Consensus. The impression that the reader gets as he continues to read the book is of finding himself before two academics who are very well intentioned but who are completely removed from the mud and blood that constitute the daily life of capitalist societies, especially in the periphery, and who have launched themselves to sail across the oceans of the empire armed with defective maps and inferior instruments of navigation. Thus, bewildered as Quixote, they take appearances as realities. Therefore, when they describe the pyramid of the empire's global constitution, Hardt and Negri assure us that: 'At the narrow pinnacle of the pyramid there is one superpower, the United States, that holds hegemony over the global use of force – a superpower that can act alone but prefers to act in collaboration with others under the umbrella of the United Nations' (p. 309).

It is very hard to understand such a naive comment, in which the sophistication expected of scientific analysis is completely lacking. To begin with, the reduction of the concept of hegemony to the use of force is inadmissible. Hegemony is much more than that. Regarding the themes of empire and imperialism, Robert Cox once wrote that hegemony could be represented as 'an adjustment among the material power, the ideology and the institutions' (Cox 1986: 225). To reduce the issue of hegemony to its military aspects only, whose importance goes beyond all doubt, is a major mistake. American hegemony is much more complex than that. On the other hand, we are told that the United States 'prefers' – surely because of its good will, its acknowledged generosity on international matters and its strict adherence to the principles of the Judeo-Christian tradition – to act in collaboration with others. One cannot help but wonder if the twenty-something pages that *Empire* devotes to a reflection upon Machiavelli's thoughts were written by the same authors that then present an interpretation of the United States' international behaviour so antithetical to the teachings of the Florentine theorist as the one I have quoted. The 'preference' of the United States – of course I am talking of the American government and its dominant classes, and not about the nation or the people of that country

– for collaborative action is merely a mask behind which the imperialist policies are adequately disguised so that they can be sold to innocent spirits. Through this operation, whose efficacy is demonstrated once again in their book, the policies of imperial expansion and domination appear as if they were real sacrifices in the name of humanity's common good. It is reasonable to suppose that the American government's top officials and their numerous ideologists and publicists could say something like this, something that not even the most submissive and servile allies of Washington would take seriously. It is entirely unreasonable for two radical critics of the system to believe these deceits.

This is not the first time that such a serious mistake appears in the book. Already in Chapter 2.5 they had written:

> In the waning years and wake of the cold war, the responsibility of exercising an international police power 'fell' squarely on the shoulders of the United States. The Gulf War was the first time the United States could exercise this power in its full form. Really, the war was an operation of repression of very little interest from the point of view of the objectives, the regional interests, and the political ideologies involved. We have seen many such wars conducted directly by the United States and its allies. Iraq was accused of having broken international law, and it thus had to be judged and punished. The importance of the Gulf War derives rather from the fact that it presented the United States as the only power able to manage international justice, *not as a function of its own national motives but in the name of global right*. (p. 180, emphasis in original)

In conclusion, and contrary to what the ancestral prejudices nurtured by the incessant anti-American preaching of the left indicate, what we learn after reading *Empire* is that poor Uncle Sam had to assume, despite his reluctance and against his will, the responsibility of exercising the role of world policeman after decades of unfruitful negotiations trying to be exempted from such a distressing obligation. Therefore, the power 'fell into' his hands while all the diplomacy of the State Department was busy in the reconstruction, on genuine democratic grounds, of the United Nations system. Meanwhile, top Washington officials travelled around the world trying to launch another round of North–South negotiations focused on reducing the irritating inequalities of the international distribution of wealth and to strengthen the languishing governments of the periphery by teaching them how to resist the exactions by which they are subdued by the gigantic transnational corporations. Those two radical scholars, lost in the darkness of theoretical confusion, find someone to give them a hand who, in the light of the day, they discover is Thomas Friedman, the very conservative editorial writer of the *New York Times* and spokesman for the opinions of the American establishment. According to Friedman, the intervention of the United States in Kosovo was legitimate (as was the one in the Gulf for other reasons) because it put an end to the ethnic cleansing practised in that region and, therefore, it was 'made in the name of global rights', to use an expression dear to Hardt and Negri. The truth is that, as Noam Chomsky has demonstrated, the ethnic cleansing of the sinister regime of Milosevic was not the cause but the consequence of the American bombings (Chomsky 2001: 81).

Let us return to the Gulf War, deplorably characterized by the authors as a 'repressive operation of scarce interest' and little importance. First of all, it is convenient to remember that this operation was not precisely a war but, as Chomsky informs us, a slaughter: 'the term "war" hardly applies to a confrontation in which one part massacres the other from an unreachable distance, while the civil society is destroyed' (Chomsky 1994: 8). The authors are not worried about this type of disquisition. Their vision of the coming of the empire with its plethora of liberating and emancipating possibilities makes their eyes look up so, for that reason, they are unaware of the horrors and miseries that current imperialist policies produce in history's mud. If the Christian theologians of the Middle Ages had their eyes completely turned to the contemplation of God and for that reason did not realize that hell was surrounding them, the authors are so dazzled by the luminous perspectives that open with the coming of the empire that the butchery inaugurated by this new historical era does not move them to write a single line of lamentation or compassion. Masters of the art of 'deconstruction', they are shown to be completely incapable of applying this resource to the analysis of a war that was in reality a massacre. They also fail to recognize, let us not say denounce, the enormous number of civilian victims of the bombing, the 'collateral damage' and the criminal embargo that followed the war. Only counting the children, the number surpasses 150,000 victims. They also remain silent about the fact that, despite his defeat, Saddam remained in power, but with the consent of the world's boss to repress at will the popular uprisings of the Kurds and the Shia minority (ibid.).

Finally, how realistic can an analysis be that considers the Gulf War, located in a zone containing the world's most important oil reserves, a matter of marginal importance for the United States? Should we think then that Washington launched its military operations moved by the imperious necessity to ensure the predominance of 'global rights' and not with the goal of reaffirming its indisputable primacy in a strategic region of the globe? Was President Bush's decision to raze Afghanistan while trying in vain to discover the whereabouts of one of its old partners, Osama Bin Laden, motivated by the need to make possible this demand for universal justice? How to describe such foolishness?

This vision of the empire's concrete functioning, and of some unpleasant events such as the Gulf War, is in line with other extremely polemic definitions made by the authors. For example, that 'the world police forces of the United States act not with an imperialistic but an imperial interest'. The grounding for this affirmation is pretty simple and refers to other passages of the book: given that imperialism has disappeared, swallowed by the commotion that destroyed the old nation-states, an intervention by the 'hegemon' makes sense only as a contribution to the stability of the empire. The pillage characteristic of the imperialistic era has been replaced by global rights and international justice.

Another issue outlined by Hardt and Negri reflects with greater clarity the serious problems that affect their vision of the really existing international system which before their eyes becomes a type of ethical empire. Thus, referring to the ascendancy that the United States achieved in the post-war world, the authors maintain that:

> With the end of the cold war, the United States was called to serve the role of guaranteeing and adding juridical efficacy to this complex process of the formation of a new supranational right. Just as in the first century of the Christian era the Roman senators asked Augustus to assume imperial powers of the administration for the public good, so too today the international monetary organizations (the United Nations, the international organizations, and even the humanitarian organizations) ask the United States to assume the central role in a new world order.
> (p. 181)

The equivocal contents of this passage of Hardt and Negri's work are very serious. First, they consider analogous two situations that are completely different: the one of the Roman Empire in the first century and the current one, when the world has changed a little – if not as much as we would like. And the old order that prevailed around the Mediterranean basin based on slavery does not seem to have many affinities with the current imperialist system that today covers the entire planet and which includes formally free populations. Second, however, is the fact that Roman senators demanding that Augustus assume imperial powers is one thing and the people subdued by the Roman yoke asking for this is another, very different, thing. Certainly, there is a considerable majority of American senators who repeatedly lobby the White House on the need for acting as an articulating and organizing axis for the benefit of the companies and national interests of the United States, as we will see in the following chapters. Another, very different thing is that people, nations and states subjected to US imperialism would demand such a thing. At this point, Hardt and Negri's analysis becomes muddled with American establishment thought because it refers to questions supposedly asked of Washington by the United Nations. When did the General Assembly request such a thing?, because this is not a matter that can be solved by an organ as little representative and anti-democratic as the Security Council; and even less by the 'international monetary organizations'. In this case, are they referring to the IMF, the World Bank, the WTO or the IDB as 'representatives' of the people's rights? What are they talking about? In any case, and even when they had reclaimed it, we know very well that such institutions are, in fact, 'informal departments' of the American government and completely lack any universal legitimacy to take up an initiative such as the one mentioned. And what can be said about the humanitarian organizations? As far as I know, neither Amnesty or the Red Cross, neither Greenpeace or the Service of Peace and Justice, or indeed any other known organization has ever formulated the petition stated in the book.

Maybe Hardt and Negri are thinking about the main role taken by the United States in the promotion of a new supranational juridical framework, which, for reasons that will soon be understood, has been conducted in secrecy by the governments involved in this enterprise. Indeed, for many years, Washington has been systematically working on the establishment of the Multilateral Agreement on Investments (MAI) and has it as a priority on its political agenda. To move forwards with this proposal, the White House counts on the always unconditional collaboration of its favourite client-state, the United Kingdom, and that of the overwhelming majority of the governments in the OECD. Among the rules that the USA has been trying to impose to consolidate universal justice and rights – surely inspired by the same literature as the authors – are two epoch-making contributions to legal science. The first is a doctrinarian innovation, thanks to which for the first time in history companies and states become juridical 'persons' enjoying exactly the same legal status. States are no longer representatives of the popular sovereignty and the nation and have become simple economic agents without any type of prerogative in the courts. It is not necessary to be a great legal scholar to be able to qualify this 'juridical advancement', zealously sought by Washington, as a phenomenal retrogression that neglects the progress made by modern law over the last three hundred years.

The second contribution: having taken into account the extraordinary concern of the American government for universal law, the MAI proposes the abolition of the reciprocity principle between the two parties signing a contract. If the MAI were approved, something that so far has not been possible thanks to tenacious opposition from humanitarian organizations and diverse social movements, one of the parties to the contract would have rights and the other one only obligations. Given the characteristics of the 'really existing' empire, it is not hard to find out who would have what: companies would have the right to take states to the courts of justice, but the states would be debarred from doing so with investors that did not comply with their obligations. Of course, given the well-known concern of the American government to guarantee universal democracy, it is permitted for a state to file a law suit against another state, with which things become more even. Thus, if the governments of Guatemala or Ecuador had a problem with United Fruit or Chiquita Banana, they would not be able to file a suit against those companies, but they would be free and would have all the guarantees in the world to do it against the government of the United States, given that, despite what Hardt and Negri think, those companies are American and are registered in that country. Now we can understand the reasons why the negotiations that ended in a draft MAI were conducted in absolute secrecy and beyond any type of democratic and popular control (Boron 2001a: 31–62; Chomsky 2000a: 259–60; Lander 1998).

Given such a huge distortion of the empire's realities, it is not surprising that the authors conclude:

> In all the regional conflicts of the late twentieth century, from Haiti to the Persian Gulf and Somalia to Bosnia, the United States is called to intervene militarily – and these calls are real and substantial, not merely publicity stunts to quell U.S. public dissent. Even if it were reluctant, the U.S. military would have to answer the call in the name of peace and order. (p. 181)

No comment.

The empire as it is, portrayed by its organic intellectuals

Hence, it seems to be sufficiently proved that Hardt and Negri's analysis of the contemporary world order is wrong, based on a seriously distorted reading of the current transformations that are taking place in state formations and in the world markets of contemporary capitalism. This is not to deny that, occasionally, here and there, the reader can find a few sharp reflections and observations related to some timely issues, but the general picture that flows from their analysis is theoretically wrong and politically self-defeating.

A good exercise that could help Hardt and Negri to descend from the structuralist nebula in which they seem to have suspended their reasoning – 'a new global form of sovereignty' (p. xii), 'a specific regime of global relations' (pp. 45–6) – would be to read the work of some of the main organic intellectuals of the empire. Leo Panitch has called attention to a meaningful paradox: while the term 'imperialism' has fallen into disuse, the realities of imperialism are more vivid and impressive than ever. This paradox is much more accute in Latin America, where not only the term 'imperialism' but also the word 'dependency' have been expelled from academic language and public discourse, precisely at a time when the subjection of Latin American countries to transnational economic forces has reached unprecedented levels. The reasons for this are many: among them the ideological and political defeat of the left and its consequences stand out. The adoption of the language of the victors and the inability to resist their blackmail, especially among those obsessed with preserving their careers and gaining 'public acknowledgement', reinforces this subjection. This phenomenon can be verified not only in Latin America but also in Europe and the United States. In Europe, it is mainly evident in those countries in which communist parties were very strong and the presence of the political left vigorous, such as in Italy, France and Spain. This is why Panitch suggests that if the left wants to face reality, maybe 'it should look to the right to obtain a clear vision of the direction in which it should march' (Panitch 2000: 18–20). Why? Because while many on the left are inclined to forget the existence of class struggles and imperialism (fearful of being denounced by the prevailing neoliberal and postmodern consensus as self-indulgent and absurd dinosaurs escaped from the Jurassic Park of socialism), the mandarins of the empire, busy as they are giving advice to the dominant classes who are faced daily by class antagonists and emancipatory struggles, have no time to waste on fantasies or poetry. The practical necessities of imperial administration do not allow them to become distracted by metaphysical lucubrations. This is one of the reasons why Zbigniew Brzezinski is so clear in his diagnosis, and instead of talking about a phantasmagoric empire, such as the one depicted by Hardt and Negri, he goes directly to the point and celebrates without shame the irresistible ascension, in his own judgement, of the United States to the condition of 'only global superpower'. Focused on assuring the long-term stability of the imperialist phase opened after the fall of the Soviet Union, Brzezinski identifies three main guiding principles of the American geopolitical strategy: first, to impede the collusion among, and to preserve the dependence of, the most powerful vassals on issues of security (Western Europe and Japan); second, to maintain the submission and obedience of the tributary nations, such as Latin America and the Third World in general; and third, to prevent the unification, the overflow and eventual attack of the 'barbarians', a denomination that embraces countries from China to Russia, including the Islamic nations of Central Asia and the Middle East (Brzezinski 1998: 40). Crystal clear.

The former US National Security Council chairman's observations offer a clear vision without beating about the bush, distant from the vague rhetoric employed by Hardt and Negri and, precisely because of this, extremely instructive of what these authors call empire and Panitch calls 'new imperialism'. In 1989, long before Brzezinski expressed these ideas, Susan Strange, not exactly a Marxist scholar, wrote an article. Had it been read by our authors, it would have saved them time and prevented them from making extremely serious mistakes. Strange said:

> What is emerging is, therefore, a non-territorial empire with its imperial capital in Washington DC. If the imperial capitals used to attract courtesans of foreign provinces, Washington instead attracts 'lobbies' and agents of the international companies, representatives of minority groups dispersed throughout the empire and pressure groups organized at a global scale. [...] As in Rome, citizenship is not limited to a superior race and the empire contains a mix of citizens with the same legal and political rights, semi-citizens and non-citizens, such as the slave population in Rome. [...] The semi-citizens of the empire are many and they are spread out. [...] They include many people employed by big transnational firms that operate in the transnational structure of production that assists, as they all well know, the global market. This includes the people employed

in transnational banking and, very often, the members of the 'national' armed forces, especially those that are trained, armed by, and dependent on the United States armed forces. It also includes many scholars in medicine, the natural sciences and the social sciences, as in business management and economy, who view the American professional associations and universities as those peers before whose eyes they want to shine and excel. It also includes the people in the press and the mass media, for whom the American technology and the examples offered by the United States have shown the way, changing the established institutions and organizations. (Strange 1989: 167)

It is unquestionable that, despite her rejection of Marxism, Strange's diagnosis of the international structure and the organization of the empire has more in common with historical materialism than the one that arises from Hardt and Negri's work. This is not the first time that a rigorous and objective liberal, thanks to the realism that informs her analysis, provides a vision that is closer to Marxist analysis than that provided by authors tacitly or outspokenly identified with that theoretical tradition. In addition to the vibrant perspective that Brzezinski and Strange have offered us, we have a crude diagnosis made by one of the most distinguished theoreticians of American neo-conservatism, Samuel P. Huntington; he also has no doubts about the imperialist character of the current world order. Huntington's concern is with the weakness and vulnerability of the USA and its condition as the 'lonely sheriff'. This condition has obliged Washington to exert a vicious international power, one of the consequences of which could be the formation of a very broad anti-American coalition including not only Russia and China but also, though in differing degrees, the European states, which could put the current world order in crisis. To refute the sceptics and refresh the memory of those who have forgotten what the imperialist relationships are, it is convenient to reproduce *in extenso* the long string of initiatives that, according to Huntington, were driven by Washington in recent years:

> To press other countries to adopt American values and practices on issues such as human rights and democracy; to prevent that third countries acquire military capacities susceptible of interfering with the American military superiority; to have the American legislation applied in other societies; to qualify third countries with regards to their adhesion to American standards on human rights, drugs, terrorism, nuclear and missile prolifera-tion and, now, religious freedom; to apply sanctions against the countries that do not conform to the American standards on these issues; to promote the corporate American interests under the slogans of free trade and open markets and to shape the politics of the IMF and the World Bank to serve those same interests; [...] to force other countries to adopt social and economic policies that benefit the American economic interests, to promote the sale of American weapons and prevent that other countries do the same [...] to categorize certain countries as 'pariah states' or criminal states and exclude them from the global institutions because they refuse to prostrate themselves before the American wishes. (Huntington 1999: 48)

Let us be clear, this is not incendiary criticism by an enemy of American imperialism, rather it is a sober account written by one of its most lucid organic intellectuals, concerned about the self-destructive trends that have arisen from America's exercise of its hegemony in a unipolar world. Given the images that arise from the work of the three authors whose ideas we have pres-ented, the sometimes poetic and at other times metaphysical dis-course of Hardt and Negri vanishes because of its own lightness and its radical disconnection with what Huntington appropriately calls the responsibilities of the 'lonely superpower'. What emerges from Hardt and Negri's analysis is that the assumed 'new form of global sovereignty' exercised by the world 'Empire', which would impose a new global logic of domination, is not a world empire but 'American logic of domination'. There is no doubt that there are supranational and transnational organizations, just as there is no doubt that behind them lies the American national interest. It is obvious that the American national interest does not exist in the abstract, nor is it in the interests of the American people or the nation. It is in the interests of the big corporate conglomerates which control as they please the government of the United States, Congress, the judicial powers, the mass media, the major universities and centres of study and the framework that allows them to retain a formidable hegemony over civil society. Institutions that are supposedly 'intergovernmental' or international, such as the IMF, the World Bank and the World Trade Organization, are at the service of corporate American interests. The interventions of the USA in other regions of the world have different motivations, but did they take place, as Hardt and Negri claim, to establish international law? In this sense, Brzezinski could not have been more categorical when he said that the so-called supranational institutions are, in fact, part of the imperial system, something that is particularly true in the case of the international financial institutions (Brzezinski 1998: 28–9).

5 The nation-state and the issue of sovereignty

As we have seen in previous chapters, according to Hardt and Negri, the constitution of the empire overlays the decadence and final, supposedly inexorable, collapse of the nation-state. According to our authors, the sovereignty that nation-states retained in the past has been transferred to a new global structure of domination in which decadent state formations play an increasingly marginal role. There are, we are assured, no imperialist players or a territorial centre of power; nor do there exist established barriers or limits or fixed identities or crystallized hierarchies. The transition from the age of imperialism, based on a collection of bellicose states in permanent conflict among themselves, to the age of the empire, is signalled by the irreversible decline of the institutional and legal foundations of the old order, the nation-state. It is because of this that Hardt and Negri plainly reject the idea that the United States is 'the ultimate authority that rules over the processes of globalization and the new world order' (p. xiii). Both those who see the United States as a lonely and omnipotent superpower, a fervent defender of freedom, and those who denounce that country as an imperialist oppressor, are wrong, Hardt and Negri say, because both parties assume that the old nation-state's sovereignty is still in force and do not realize that it is a relic of the past. Unaware of this mutation they also fail to understand that imperialism is over (ibid.).

Let us examine some of the problems that this interpretation poses. In the first place, let us say that to assume that there can exist something like an authority able to govern 'all the processes of globalization and the new world order' is not an innocent mistake. Why? Because given such a requirement the only sensible answer is to deny the existence of such an authority. To say that a certain structure of power can control all the processes that occur in its jurisdiction is absurd. Not even the most elementary forms of organization of social power, such as the ones reported by anthropologists studying 'primitive hordes', were capable of fulfilling such a requirement. Fortunately, the omnipotence of the powerful does not exist. There are always loopholes and, invariably, there will be things that the power cannot control. Even in the most extreme cases of despotic concentrations of power – Nazi Germany or some of the most oppressive and ferocious Latin American dictatorships such as Videla's in Argentina, Pinochet's in Chile, Trujillo's in the Dominican Republic and Somoza's in Nicaragua – the authorities at the time demonstrated an incapacity to control 'all the processes' unfolding in their countries. To say that there is no imperialism because there is no one who can take control at a world level – a world whose complexity transcends the limits of our imagination – constitutes a dismissive statement. It is a question of finding out if in the new world order, so celebrated by George Bush Senior after the Gulf War, there are some players who hold an extraordinarily elevated share of power and whose interests prevail systematically. It is a question of examining whether the design of this new world reflects, somehow, the asymmetric distribution of power that existed in the old world, and how it works. Of course, to talk about an 'extraordinarily elevated' share of power is to admit that there are others who have some power, and if we speak of systematic predominance it is also accepted that there may be some deviations that, from time to time, will produce unexpected results.

This being said, let us continue with a second problem. Hardt and Negri's analysis of the issue of sovereignty is wrong, as is their interpretation of the changes experienced by social structures in recent times. Regarding the issue of sovereignty, they seem not to have noticed that in the imperialist structure there is a yardstick of evaluation, or, as Jeane Kirkpatrick, the US Ambassador to the

United Nations during Ronald Reagan's first term, said, there is a *double standard* with which Washington judges foreign governments and their actions. One standard is used to evaluate the sovereignty of the friends and allies of the United States; another, very different, is used to judge the sovereignty of neutral countries and its enemies. The national sovereignty of the former must be preserved and strengthened, the latter's should be weakened and violated without scruples or false regrets. Prisoners of their own speculations, Hardt and Negri cannot perceive this disturbing duality, believing thus that there is a 'global logic' beyond and above the national interest of the superpower and undeniable 'centre' of the empire, the United States. For authors so interested in constitutional and juridical matters, as is the case of Hardt and Negri, the deplorable performance of Washington regarding the acknowledgement of international treaties and agreements provides a timely douche of sobriety. As is well known, the United States has repudiated any international juridical instrument that implies even a minimal reduction of its sovereignty. Recently, Washington has deliberately delayed agreeing to the constitution of an International Criminal Court sited in Rome – with special competence to judge war crimes, crimes against humanity and genocide – because this would mean a transference of sovereignty to an international organ whose control could escape from their hands. The United States actively participated in all the previous deliberations about setting up the court, it discussed criteria, it vetoed norms and co-authored various drafts of the constitution. But when the time came to approve the constitution of the court in Rome, it decided to walk away.

This should come as no surprise to students of imperialism, though it seems to have confused the authors of *Empire*. Apparently, they have ignored the fact that the United States has one of the worst world records regarding the ratification of international conventions and agreements, precisely because Washington considers that these would be detrimental to American national sovereignty and its interests as a superpower. Recently, the USA refused to sign the Kyoto Agreement to preserve the environment, using the argument that it would harm the profits of American companies. In the case of the International Convention on the Rights of the Child, only two countries in the whole world refused to sign the protocol: Somalia and the United States. But as pointed out by Noam Chomsky, actually the United States 'have not ratified a single convention, because even in the very few cases in which they did so, the American government managed to introduce a reserve clause that says the following: "not applicable to the United States without the consensus of the United States"' (Chomsky 2001: 63).

In the neo-conservative zenith of the 1980s, the United States refused (and in some cases is still refusing) to pay its fees to some of the main agencies of the United Nations, accusing them of having defied American sovereignty. Why pay membership fees to an institution that Washington cannot control at will? A similar attitude is observed in relation to another US creation, the WTO, and its preceding agreement, the GATT. The European Union accused the American government of damaging European companies because the embargo against Cuba violated the commercial rules previously agreed. Besides, the European Union said, the embargo was immoral, it had been unanimously condemned and children and the elderly were its main victims. The embargo's unfavourable impact on health and nutrition policies as well as other similar considerations were also highlighted. The response from Washington was that these were not commercial or humanitarian issues but, instead, they were matters related to American national security and, therefore, they would not be transferred to any other international agency or institution but would be exclusively managed by the different branches of the American government without allowing any, even minimal, foreign intervention (ibid.: 64–6).

A final example will be useful to conclude this discussion.

During the offensive of the Nicaraguan Contras – illegally armed, trained, financed and organized by the United States – the government of Managua filed a demand in 1985 to the International Court of Justice accusing the American government of war crimes against the Nicaraguan civil population. The response from Washington was to disregard the court's jurisdiction. The process continued anyway, and the final sentence of the court ordered Washington to stop its military operations, retire the mercenary forces stationed in Nicaragua and pay substantial reparations to compensate for the damage inflicted on the civil society. The government of the United States simply disregarded the sentence, continued the war, whose results are well known, and not even when it managed to instal a new 'friendly' government in Nicaragua did it dare to sit down to talk about the reparations of war, let alone paying them. The same occurred with Vietnam. These are good examples of what Hardt and Negri understand as the imperial creation of 'global rights' and the empire of universal justice (ibid.: 69–70).

It seems clear that the authors have not managed to appreciate the continuous relevance of national sovereignty, the national interest and national power in all its magnitude, all of which incurably weakens the central hypothesis of their argument that insists there is a global and abstract logic that presides over the functioning of the empire. Regarding what occurred with the capitalist state in its current phase, it seems that the mistakes cited before become even more serious. First of all, there is an important initial problem that is not marginal at all, with respect to the proclaimed final and irreversible decadence of the state: all the available quantitative information with regard to public expenditure and the size of the state apparatus moves in the opposite direction of the one imagined by Hardt and Negri. If something has occurred in metropolitan capitalisms in the last twenty years, it has been precisely the noticeable increase of the size of the state, measured as the proportion of public expenditures to GDP. The information provided by all types of sources, from national governments to the United Nations Development Programme (UNDP), and from the World Bank to the IMF and the OECD, speak with a single voice: all the states of the metropolitan capitalisms were strengthened in the last twenty years, despite the fact that many of the governments in those states have been veritable champions of the anti-state rhetoric that was launched with fury at the beginning of the 1980s. What happened after the crisis of Keynesian capitalism in the middle of the 1970s was a relative decrease in the growth rate of public expenditure. Fiscal budgets continued to grow uninterruptedly, although at more modest levels than before. That is why a special report on this topic in the conservative British magazine *The Economist* (1997) is entitled 'Big Government is Still in Charge'. The writer of this article cannot hide his disappointment at the states' tenacious resistance to becoming smaller as mandated by the neoliberal catechism. (Hardt and Negri seem not to have examined this work because the last section of Chapter 3.6 in their book is entitled 'Big Government is Over!', a heading that clearly reflects the extent of their misunderstanding of a theme so crucial to their theoretical argument.) In any case, after a careful analysis of recent data on public expenditure in fourteen industrialized countries of the OECD, *The Economist* concludes that, despite the neoliberal reforms initiated after the proclaimed new goals of fiscal austerity and public expenditure reduction between 1980 and 1996, public expenditure in the selected countries grew from 43.3 per cent of the GDP to 47.1 per cent, while in countries such as Sweden this figure passes the 50 per cent threshold: 'in the last forty years the growth of public expenditure in the developed economies has been persistent, universal and counterproductive', and the objective so strongly proclaimed of becoming a 'small government' apparently has been more a weapon of electoral rhetoric than a true objective of economic policy. Not even the strongest defenders of the famous 'state reform' and the shrinking of public expenditure, such as Ronald Reagan and Margaret Thatcher, managed to achieve any significant progress in this terrain.

Thus, if this strengthening of state organizations is verified in the heart of developed capitalisms, the history of the periphery is completely different. In the international reorganization of the imperialist system under the ideological shield of neoliberalism, states were radically weakened and the economies of the periphery were subdued to become more and more open, and almost without any state mediation, to the influx of the great transnational companies and to the policies of the developed countries, mainly the United States. This process was in no way a natural one, but instead was the result of initiatives adopted at the centre of the empire: the government of the United States, in its role as ruler, accompanied by its loyal guard dogs (the IMF, the World Bank, the WTO, etc.) and supported by the active complicity of the countries of the G-7. This coalition forced (in many cases brutally) the indebted countries of the Third World to apply the policies known as the 'Washington Consensus' and to transform their economies in accordance with the interests of the dominant coalition and, especially, of the *primus inter pares*, the United States. These policies favoured the practically unlimited penetration of American and European corporate interests into the domestic markets of the southern nations. For that to take place, it was necessary to dismantle the public sector in those countries, produce a real deconstruction of the state and, with the aim of generating surplus for the payment of these countries' foreign debt, to reduce public expenditure to the minimum, sacrificing in this way vital and impossible-to-postpone expenditure on health, housing and education. State-owned companies were first financially drained and then sold at ridiculous prices to the big corporations of the central countries, thereby creating a space for the maximum exercise of 'private initiative'. (Despite that, in many cases, the buyers were state-owned companies from the industrialized countries.) Another policy imposed on these countries was the unilateral opening up of the economy, facilitating an invasion of imported goods produced in other countries while the unemployment rates increased exponentially. It is pertinent to state that while the periphery was forced to open up commercially, protectionism in the North became more sophisticated. The deregulation of markets, especially the financial one, was another of the objectives of the 'capitalist revolution' in the 1980s. All together, these policies had the result of dramatically weakening the states of the periphery, while fulfilling the capitalist dream of having markets operating without state regulation, as a result of which the strongest corporate conglomerates actually took charge of 'regulating' the market, obviously in their own interests. As I said before, these policies were not fortuitous or accidental, given that the dismantling of the states increased significantly the ability of imperialism and foreign companies and nations to control not only the economic life but also the political life of the countries of the periphery. Of course, we find nothing of this in *Empire*. What we do find, instead, are reiterative passages claiming that imperialist relationships have ended, despite the fact that the visibility they have acquired in recent decades is so striking that even the least radical sectors of our societies have no trouble in recognizing them.

A concrete example of the consequences of this acute weakening of the state in the capitalisms of the periphery has been stressed by Honduran historian Ramón Oquelí. Referring to his country in the mid-1980s, with its well-established democratic regime, Oquelí observed:

> The importance of the presidential elections, with or without fraud, is relative. The decisions that affect Honduras are first made in Washington; then in the American military command in Panamá (the Southern Command); afterwards in the American base command of Palmerola, Honduras; immediately

after in the American Embassy in Tegucigalpa; in the fifth place comes the commander-in-chief of the Honduran armed forces; and the president of the Republic only appears in sixth place. We vote, then, for a sixth-category official in terms of decision capacity. The president's functions are limited to managing misery and obtaining American loans. (Cueva 1986: 50)

Replace Honduras with almost any other Latin American country and a similar picture will emerge. Obviously, the predominant military situation in those years assigned the armed forces a very special role. For the countries that do not face a serious military crisis, that central role today falls into the hands of the Treasury and the IMF, and the president can, in such a case, move up the decision ladder to the third or fourth rung, but no further than that. Regarding the president's main functions – managing misery and obtaining American loans – things have not changed. The Argentine case is a shining example of all this.

Continuing with the *problematique* of the state, our authors do not seem able to distinguish between state forms and functions and the tasks of states. There is no doubt that the form of the capitalist state has changed in the last quarter of a century. Since the state is not a metaphysical entity but a historical creature, continually formed and reformed by class struggles, its forms can hardly be interpreted as immanent essences floating above the historical process. Consequently, the forms of the democratic state in the developed capitalist countries have changed. How? There has been real democratic degeneration: a progressive loss of power formerly in the hands of congresses and parliaments; the growing unaccountability of governments, which goes hand-in-hand with the increasing concentration of power in the hands of executives; the proliferation of secret areas of decision-making (see, for example, the aborted negotiations of the MAI, the accelerated approval of the NAFTA, the current negotiations behind closed doors to create the Free Trade Area of the Americas); declining levels of governmental response to the claims and demands of civil society; a drastic reduction of competition among political parties because of increasing similarities between the majority political parties, following the bipartisan American model; the tyranny of the markets – in fact, of the oligopolies that control them – that vote every day and capture the permanent attention of the governments while the public votes every two or three years; related to the aforementioned, logical trends towards political apathy and individualist retraction; the growing predominance of the big oligopolies in the mass media and the cultural industry; and, lastly, an increasing transference of the right to make decisions from popular sovereignty to the administrative and political agencies of the empire, a process that exists both in the empire's 'exterior provinces' and in its centre. In the Latin American case this means that popular sovereignty has been deprived of almost all its attributes, and that no strategic decision on economic or social matters is adopted in these countries without previous consultation with, and the approval of, the relevant agency in Washington. As we can see, a situation like this cannot but contradict the essence of the democratic order, and popular sovereignty is reduced to a mere dead letter.

Boaventura de Sousa Santos has examined the changes experienced by states under neoliberal globalization and his analysis confirms that 'there is by no means an overall crisis of the state, let alone a terminal crisis of the state, such as suggested by the most extreme theses of globalization scholars' (de Sousa Santos 1999: 64). The Hobbesian repressive functions of the state enjoy their vigour both in the periphery and in the centre of the system. In the former, because the implementation of strongly repressive policies has become necessary to prop up an increasingly unjust and unequal capitalist organization, where the numbers of the exploited and the excluded increase incessantly. In the centre, on the other hand, because this occurs especially in the United States, a significant proportion of their social problems is dealt with by channelling people towards the prison system, though this situation also occurs, but less acutely, in other countries. It is estimated that today the total number of prisoners in America amounts to a figure only surpassed by the populations of the three major cities of that country, New York, Chicago and Los Angeles, and that the overwhelming majority of the convicts are black or Latino. As de Sousa Santos correctly notes, in the social apartheid of contemporary capitalism the state continues to perform a crucial role: it is the Hobbesian Leviathan in the ghettos and the marginal neighbourhoods while it guarantees the benefits of the social Lockean contract for those who inhabit the opulent suburbs. Consequently, this state supposedly on the way to becoming extinct, according to the obfuscated vision of Hardt and Negri, continues on its way as a divided state, almost schizophrenic: for the poor and the excluded, a fascist state; for the rich, a democratic state. But the vitality of the nation-state is not measured only in these terms; it can also be proved by the role it plays in several other fields, such as supranational unification, the liberalization of the economy, the commercial opening up, the deregulation of the financial system and the elaboration of an institutional-juridical framework adequate for the protection of private companies and the new economic model inspired by the 'Washington Consensus'. 'What is in crisis is the function of promoting non-mercantile exchanges among citizens,' concludes de Sousa Santos (ibid.: 64).

As Ellen Meiskins Wood (2000: 116) demonstrates, the nation-state continues to be the main agent of globalization. In the global markets, the need that capital has for the state is even more pronounced than before. A recent analysis shows that in the processes of economic restructuring, the national states of metropolitan capitalisms, far from being the 'victims' of globalization, were its main promoters. The international expansion of the financial, industrial and commercial capital of the United States, the European countries, Japan, South Korea, Singapore and Taiwan 'was not a macroeconomic phenomenon born inside the companies' but, instead, was the product of a political strategy directed at improving the relative position of those countries in the changing international economic scene. In this strategy, actors such as the US Treasury, the MITI of Japan, the European Commission and a group of national state agencies played a central role (Weiss 1997: 23). This is why Peter Drucker, one of the most prestigious US gurus, calls our attention to the amazing persistence of states despite the great changes that occurred in the world economy and he concludes that they will, for sure, survive the globalization of the economy and the information technology revolution (Drucker 1997: 160).

It seems appropriate to quote what one of the major advocates of US imperialism has written on these issues, ratifying the key role played by the capitalist states, and very especially the American state, in globalization. 'As the country that benefits most from global economic integration, we have the responsibility of making sure that this new system is sustainable [...] Sustaining globalization is our overarching national interest,' says Thomas Friedman. And the implications of the fact that 'globalization-is-US' the *New York Times* columnist does not fail to notice that 'because we are the biggest beneficiaries and drivers of globalization, we are unwittingly putting enormous pressure on the rest of the world' (Friedman 1999).

To sum up: the global markets strengthen competition between the giant corporations that dominate the global economy. Since these companies are transnational in their reach and the range of their operations while still possessing a national base, in order to succeed in this relentless battle they require the support of 'their governments' to keep their commercial rivals in line. Aware of this, the national states offer 'their companies' a menu of alternatives which include the following: the concession of direct subsidies for national companies; the gigantic rescue operations of banks and companies, paid in many cases through taxes applied to workers and consumers; the imposition of fiscal austerity policies and structural adjustment programmes directed towards guaranteeing greater profit rates for the companies; the devaluation or appreciation of the local currency, in order to favour some fractions of capital while placing the burden of the crisis on other sectors and social groups; the deregulation of markets; the implementation of 'labour reforms' intended to accentuate the submission of workers, weakening both their capacity to negotiate their wages and their labour unions; the enforcement of the international immobility of workers while facilitating the international mobility of capital; the guarantee of 'law and order' in societies that experience regressive social processes of wealth and income re-concentration and massive processes of pauperization; the creation of a legal framework capable of ratifying favourable terms and opportunities that companies have enjoyed in the current phase; and the establishment of a legislation that 'legalizes', in the countries of the periphery, the imperialist suction of surplus-value and that allows for the great profits of the transnational companies to be freely remitted to their headquarters. These are some of the tasks that the national states perform and that the 'global logic of the Empire', so exalted in Hardt and Negri's analysis, can guarantee only through the still indispensable mediation of the nation-state (Meiskins Wood 2000: 116–17). That the most prominent and influential members of the capitalist class are actively working to destroy such a useful and formidable instrument as the nation-state can be understood only by assuming that the capitalist class is made up of idiots (I must state right away, to clear up possible doubts, that the capitalist state is not only an instrument of the bourgeoisie but also many other things, which do not prevent it from also being an indispensable instrument in the process of capital accumulation).[1] In light of this, Ellen Meiskins Wood concludes:

---

1 I have examined this issue in detail in Boron (1995).

Of course, it is possible for the state to change its form, and for the traditional nation-state to give room, on the one hand, to most strictly local states and, on the other hand, to wider regional political authorities. But regardless of its shape, the state will still be crucial, and it is likely that for a long time even the old nation-state will continue to play its dominant role. (Meiskins Wood 2000: 117)

6 The unsolved mystery of the multitude

Obsessive denial of the realities of the nation-state leads Hardt and Negri to a political dead-end. Let us review, therefore, a passage from *Empire* that I analysed from another perspective in Chapter 5. In that chapter I said that, together with the terminal crisis of the state, Hardt and Negri also observed 'the decline [...] of any independent space where revolution could emerge in the national political regime, or where social space could be transformed using the instruments of the state' (pp. 307–8). Consequently, without the oxygen provided by that space, the flame of revolution is extinguished. If this is true, how can one break the iron cage of the empire? The answer offered by the authors is silence. The word 'revolution' is mentioned only five or six times in the thick volume under analysis, and the subject occupies a lot less space than the ten pages assigned to the study of population mobility or the eleven pages devoted to a discussion of republicanism. How can such noisy silence be understood?

The vague references to 'the multitude' in the final chapter of *Empire* do not offer any clues as to how this oppressive world order – much more oppressive than the preceding one, it should be remembered – may some day be transcended. The problem is not only that the references to the multitude are vague. Michael Hardt acknowledged in a recent interview that, 'in our book the concept of multitude works as a poetic concept rather than as a factual one' (Cangi 2002: 3). Hardt is right about that, because such a notion is, sociologically speaking, empty, though it is necessary to recognize that it has a considerable poetic force which makes it extremely attractive. We are told that the multitude is the totality of the creative and productive subjectivities that 'express, nourish, and develop positively their own constituent projects' and that they 'work toward the liberation of living labor, creating constellations of powerful singularities' (p. 61). Thus, with a stroke of the pen, social classes disappear from the scene and the distinction between exploiters and exploited and between the weak and the powerful evaporates. What is left after this shadowy operation is an amorphous mass of highly creative singularities that, if existent, would put the thesis of the alienating character of labour and daily life in capitalist societies in serious trouble. If we applied Hardt and Negri's work to the prosaic reality of contemporary Latin America, we should ask ourselves if the paramilitaries and death squads that razed Chiapas and a good part of Central America, sowing terror and death, are included in the multitude; or the landowners who organize and finance a great part of the private repression exerted in those countries against peasants and aboriginal communities; or the financial speculators and the bourgeoisie who supported military regimes in the past and who today undermine the languishing democracies. Does this category include those who, in the name of capital, control the cultural industry of Latin America at their pleasure? Do humiliated and exploited peasants, blacks, Indians, cholos and mestizos form part of the multitude too? And what about the urban 'proletariat' sunk in exclusion and misery, the workers and the unemployed, the single mothers and overexploited women, the sexual minorities, the children of the streets, the pauperized elderly, public employees and the impoverished middle classes? If they are not in this category, where can this vast conglomerate be placed socially? And if they indeed share their place in the multitude with the social agents of exploitation and repression, what sense is there in using such a category? What is it that it describes, to say nothing of what it could explain? *Empire* does not offer any such explanations. It is, as Hardt said in the interview mentioned above, a poetic concept. But poetry is not always useful for explaining reality, or for changing it. Sometimes, good poetry makes bad sociology, and this seems to be the case here.

Leaving aside these disagreeable observations, the programme proposed for the multitude is explained in the final chapter of the book. The combination of the basic precepts of the neoliberal theory of globalization and a sociologically amorphous concept such as that of the 'multitude' results in a cautiously reform-ist political programme and, to make things worse, not a very realistic one. An 'abstract internationalism' permeates it and this results in what the authors call the 'first element of a political program for the global multitude, a first political demand: *global citizenship*' (p. 400, emphasis in original). I cannot disagree with this claim, an old aspiration already proposed by Kant and that Marx and Engels recovered and redefined within the framework of the internationalism proclaimed with so much vigour in the *Manifesto*. But citizenship has always involved a set of rights and prerogatives as well as requiring the creation of adequate chan-nels of political participation that, to be effective and not illusory, must be realized within a legal and institutional framework such as, in recent history, was provided by the nation-state. Whoever speaks of citizenship, speaks of power, relationships of force, and the state as the basic framework within which a juridical order is elaborated and supported. Since, according to Hardt and Negri, the state faces an irreversible decline, within what framework is the emancipating and participative potential of the citizenship to be realized? 'Abstract internationalism' believes that the solution for most of our problems lies in the empowerment of civil society and the construction of a global and cosmopolitan citizenship. The problem is that, in its arrogant abstraction, this interna-tionalism relies on 'an abstract and little realistic notion of an international civil society or global citizenship' and on the illusion that the world can be changed if the representation of the left and the popular movements – let us say for a moment, the multitude – are strengthened within the large transnational organizations such as the IMF (Meiskins Wood 2000: 118). Though the argument developed in *Empire* is not very clear about this, it seems, however, to be in line with a certain type of reasoning that in recent years has acquired great popularity thanks to the efforts of a wide range of intellectuals and 'experts' connected to the World Bank and other international financial institutions. The proposals outline, especially in the framework of national societies, the beginning of a process of 'devolution' to civil society functions that had been improperly appropriated by the state. Obviously, these policies are 'the other side of the coin' of the privatizations and the dismantling of the public sector that the international financial institutions have promoted over the last twenty years. Such changes seek to provide a solution to the crisis triggered by the state's desertion of its responsibilities in the provision of public welfare – providing social assistance, education, healthcare and so on – transferring to civil society the task of dealing with these issues while incidentally preserving a balanced fiscal budget and, eventually, guaranteeing the existence of a surplus in the fiscal accounts in order to fund the foreign debt. If this policy of empowerment of civil society is unrealistic at the national level, its transference to the international level deepens the cracks apparent in its own foundations. The so-called global civil society, far from being liberated from class limitations that make impossible the full expansion of citizens' rights in national societies, suffers from these same limitations even more acutely, riddled as it is by abysmal economic and social inequalities and by the oppressive features inscribed in its structures, norms and rules of operation. If democracy and citizenship have proved to be such elusive and practically ungraspable objectives in the capitalisms of the periphery, why should we expect them to be obtainable in the even less unfavourable terrain of the international system?

The price that Hardt and Negri pay for ignoring this is the extreme naivety of their proposal, closer to a religious exhortation than to a realistic social-democratic demand. According to it, capitalists should acknowledge that capital is created by the workers and, therefore, accept 'in postmodernity [...] the fundamental modern constitutional principle that links right and labor, and thus rewards with citizenship the worker who creates capital' (p. 400). The multitude's emancipation, consequently, seems to run along the following course: 'If in a first moment the multitude demands that each state recognize juridically the migrations that are necessary to capital, in a second moment it must demand control over the movements themselves' (p. 400). Consequently, our authors conclude: '*The general right to control its own movement is the multitude's ultimate demand for global citizenship*' (p. 400, emphasis in original). It is of no use to search the book for a discussion of the reasons why large numbers of our people have to emigrate, desperately seeking to be exploited in the metropolitan capitalisms, since the destruction – sometimes the silent genocide – practised in the periphery and the deterioration of every form of civilized life under the rise of neoliberalism are completely absent from the pages of *Empire*. Similarly useless would be the search for a serious discussion about the reach and limitations that migration and a nomadic way of life would have in a (revolutionary?) project that would allow the multitudes to take control of their lives; putting an end to the slavery of waged labour and of nomimally 'free' subjects throughout the world. Because of this, the equation between migration/nomadism and liberation/revolution acquires illusory characteristics.

The second component of the supposedly emancipating programme of the multitude in its effort to defeat the empire is the right to a social wage and a guaranteed minimum income for everybody. This demand goes one step beyond the family wage, putting an end to the unpaid labour of workers' wives and family members. The distinction between productive and reproductive labour fades in the biopolitical context of the empire, since it is the multitude in its totality that produces and reproduces the social life. Thus, 'The demand for a social wage extends to the entire population the demand that all activity necessary for the production of capital be recognized with an equal compensation such that a social wage is really a guaranteed income' (p. 403). Once again, fine intentions with which everybody can agree. But it is pertinent to formulate some questions: first, is not this second component of the emancipating programme extremely similar to the 'citizens' wage' that, with some restrictions it is true, has been conceded in some of the most advanced industrialized democracies of the North? Is it so different from the moderate social-democrat reformism in place in some of the Scandinavian countries, especially Sweden? It does not seem so. Instead, it appears that this would be the deepening of a trend going back almost half a century without, at least as seen from here, having checkmated the capitalists or neutralized the exploitative character of the bourgeois relationships of production. Authors such as Samuel Bowles and Herbert Gintis, for example, thoroughly examined different international experiences with what they called 'the citizens' wage' without being able to infer from their analysis a conclusion that allows us to support the thesis that in states in which such a wage has been established – with greater or lesser radicalism – the multitude has been emancipated (Bowles and Gintis 1982, 1986). Second: how would the capitalist class respond to the implementation of a measure such as the aforementioned, which, despite its limitations, has an enormous distributive cost? Would they accept it without ferocious resistance? This leads, obviously, to a discussion that postmodern thinkers abhor but which imposes itself with the same unavoidable power as the universal law of gravity. We are talking, with Machiavelli, about the problematic of power and how it is obtained, exerted and lost.

The third political demand of the multitude is the right to reappropriation. It is a right that contains diverse dimensions, from language, communication and knowledge to machines, and from biopolitics to the conscience. This last component is particularly problematic because it 'deals directly with the constituent power of the multitude – or really with the product of the creative imagination of the multitude that configures its own constitution' (p. 406). On this point, which covers as we know a crucial topic in Negri's thought, such as the constituent power, the authors incessantly travel between the constitution of the multitude as a social actor – and here a wide space opens in which to discuss to what extent this process can be interpreted as the only result of its 'creative imagination' – and the constitution of the United States as it appears, in a particularly idealized fashion and, for a moment, naively interpreted, by the authors. This becomes evident when, for example, they say: 'the postmodern multitude takes away from the US Constitution what allowed it to become, above and against all other constitutions, an imperial constitution: its notion of a boundless frontier of freedom and its definition of an open spatiality and temporality celebrated in a constituent power' (p. 406).

There are a few little problems with this interpretation. First, the belief that the so-called postmodern multitude knows the American constitution or something like it, its debates and its lessons; in the best of all possible worlds this is still a remote possibility. If under the label of 'multitude' Hardt and Negri include the more than two billion people who barely survive on one or two dollars a day and without access to potable water, sewerage systems, electricity and telephones, without food or housing, it is somewhat hard to understand how they manage to imbibe the marvellous emancipating teachings of the US constitution. If, on the contrary, the authors are referring to the graduate students of Duke or Paris, then the chances improve, though not greatly. But these are minor details. The serious issue is their idealization of the American constitution. Noam Chomsky has argued repeatedly that this document, so admired by the authors of *Empire*, was conceived 'to keep the rabble in line' and to prevent them from, even by accident or by mistake, having the idea (let alone the practical possibility) that they might want to rule the destiny of the United States or even govern themselves. The American constitution is decisively and consciously anti-democratic and anti-popular, in accordance with what its most important original architects repeatedly declared. For James Madison, the main task of the constitution was that of 'assuring the supremacy of the permanent interests of the country, that are no others than the property rights'. This opinion from one of its writers probably went unnoticed by Hardt and Negri, but its force obliges us seriously to redefine the role that they assign to the US constitution, especially when we consider that Madison's words were pronounced in a country that at the time had a great part of its territory organized as a slave economy, and that the idea of the incipient constitution becoming a beacon for the emancipation of the multitude of the day, mainly slaves, apparently did not enter his thoughts. Moreover, to avoid attacks on the rights of property, Madison shrewdly designed a political system that discouraged popular participation (something that persists today, with a very low turn-out for elections which, on top of everything else, are held on working days), and fragmented the process of decision-making, while he reaffirmed the institutional balances that would guarantee that power would remain firmly in the hands of those who controlled the wealth of the country. As Chomsky observes, these opinions of Madison in the constitutional debate of Philadelphia are less well known than those expressed in the famous *Federalist Papers*, but they may be more revealing of the true spirit of the constitution than the formal declarations voiced to the general public. It is no coincidence that, as the brilliant MIT linguist remarks, in a country where the publishing industry is so dynamic, the most recent edition of those debates dates from 1838. The American people was not supposed to know about the ideas these gentlemen discussed in the convention (Boron 2000b: 228). In short, the constitution of the United States could hardly be an invitation to travel through 'the infinite frontiers of freedom', as the authors naively proclaim, since still today, and despite successive reforms (one of which prohibited the consumption of alcoholic beverages), it prevents the American multitude from directly electing their president. Thanks to the norms and procedures established in this much-admired constitution, during the last presidential election the candidate who came second in terms of the number of votes cast by the citizenship could legally become president. Apparently, the authors had not noticed the dangers lurking within the constitutional text. Malcolm Bull (2003: 85) is surely right when he asserts that: 'Although hailed by Slavoj Zizek as "the Communist Manifesto for our time", *Empire* is more Jeffersonian than Marxist.' I would add that the book is *much more* Jeffersonian than Marxist.

Another serious problem emerging from the issue of the rights of appropriation is the following: Hardt and Negri stand on solid ground when they write: 'The right to reappropriation is first of all the right to the reappropriation of the means of production' (p. 406). The old socialists and communists, they say, demanded that the proletariat should have free access to the machines and materials needed in the production process. But since one of the distinctive signs of postmodernity is the coming of what Hardt and Negri call 'the immaterial and biopolitical production', the concrete contents of the old left and the labour unions' demands have been transformed. Now the multitude not only uses machines for production but, according to the authors, it 'also becomes increasingly machinic itself, as the means of production are increasingly integrated into the minds and bodies of the multitude' (p. 406). The consequence of this mutation is that a genuine reappropriation requires free access and control over not only machines and equipment but also over 'knowledge, information, communications, and affects – because these are some of the primary means of biopolitical production' (p. 407). Now, let us analyse two not very trivial inconveniencies that emerge from the preceding argument. First, how do the knowledge, the information, the communication and the affects relate to the 'classic' material means of production and the materials that are still required to produce most of the goods necessary to sustain life on this planet? Or are we in the presence of autonomized segments of the postmodern biopolitical production? Are those segments or instruments available for anyone? Are the knowledge, the information and the communication capable of circulating freely through all classes, social strata and groups of the empire? How can the growing monopolistic features acquired by the information and mass communication industries all over the world be explained? And regarding knowledge, what can be said about patents and the crucial issue of intellectual property rights, a new method of pillage in the hands of the main transnational companies of the industrialized countries that are looting entire continents with the active support of their governments?

Second, do we have to assume that the owners and/or those who control these new and very complex and expensive means of production will peacefully and gently yield their property and its control, throwing overboard the basis of their wealth and political domination itself? Why would they act in such a way, unprecedented in the millenary history of class struggles? Would they be led to do this because their hearts would become tender before the shining vision of the self-constituted multitude marching jubilantly towards its liberation? If this is not the case, which recommendation would our authors make regarding the unavoidable intensification of class struggles and the political repression that would surely follow as a response to the emancipating initiatives of the multitude?

The fourth dimension of the political programme of the multitude is the organization of the multitude as a political subject, as *posse*. The authors introduce here the Latin word *posse* to refer to power as a verb, an activity. Thus, *posse* 'is what a body and what a mind can do' (p. 408). In the postmodern society, the constituent power of labour can be expressed as the egalitarian right of citizenship in the world or as the right to communicate, construct languages and control the communication networks; and also as a political power, which is to say, 'as the constitution of a society in which the basis of power is defined by the expression of the needs of all' (p. 410). Due to the latter, Hardt and Negri conclude with a surprisingly triumphant tone, 'The capacity to construct places, temporalities, migrations, and new bodies already affirms its hegemony through the actions of the multitude against Empire' (p. 411). They warn, though, that a small difficulty still persists: 'The only event that we are still awaiting is the construction, or rather the insurgence, of a powerful organization' (p. 411). Sensibly they recognize that they have no model to offer regarding this organization, but they are confident that 'the multitude through its practical experimentation will offer the models and determine when and how the possible becomes real' (p. 411). Some clues, however, were provided in an earlier chapter where we read that 'The real heroes of the liberation of the Third World today may really have been the emigrants and the flows of population that have destroyed old and new boundaries. Indeed, the postcolonial hero is the one who continually transgresses territorial and racial boundaries, who destroys particularisms and points toward a common civilization' (pp. 362–3). This is an enigmatic statement because it obliquely induces us to think, first, that the Third World has already achieved its liberation; second, that the multitudes of the Third World have also succeeded in their attempt to liberate themselves (an amazing revelation for four-fifths of the world population); third, that the hero of such a great deed is the migrant who abandons his native land to enter Europe or the United States, in most cases illegally, in search of a better life. The alchemy of theory has converted emigration to revolution.

7 Notes for a sociology of revolutionary thinking in times of defeat

Empire concludes with a political programme for the multitude, whose most important features have been outlined in the previous chapter. Once again, the fragility of the analysis manages to debunk both their very good intentions and their noble goals. The appendix at the end of the last chapter is extraordinarily eloquent, since it discusses the issue of political activism and finishes with a hallucinatory reference to St Francis.

This brief *excursus* begins very nicely, with the assertion that today's political activist is in no way similar to the 'sad, ascetic agent of the Third International whose soul was deeply permeated by Soviet state reason' (p. 411). On the contrary, today's activist is inspired by the image of the 'communist and liberatory combatants of the twentieth-century revolutions' (p. 412), among whom we must include those intellectuals who were persecuted and exiled during the fascist era, the republicans of the Spanish civil war, the members of the anti-fascist resistance, and those who fought for freedom in the anti-colonialist and anti-imperialist wars. The mission of the political activist has always been, and today more than ever, to organize and act, and not to represent. It is precisely their constitutive activity and not their representative activity that characterizes them. 'Militancy today is a positive, constructive, and innovative activity [...] Militants resist imperial command in a creative way' (p. 413). The culmination of this line of reasoning, nevertheless, does not lead the reader to Che Guevara or Fidel Castro, nor to Nelson Mandela, Ho Chi Minh, Mao Zedong or Ben Bella, but to St Francis of Assisi. According to Hardt and Negri, St Francis denounced the poverty that was striking the multitude of his time, and he adopted it as one of the rules of the begging order that he would later found, discovering in poverty

> the ontological power of a new society. The communist militant does the same, identifying in the common condition of the multitude its enormous wealth. Francis in opposition to nascent capitalism refused every type of instrumental discipline, and in opposition to the mortification of the flesh (in poverty and in the constituted order) he posed a joyous life, including all of being and nature, the animals, sister moon, brother sun, the birds of the field, the poor and exploited humans, together against the will of power and corruption. (p. 413)

In the postmodern world, Hardt and Negri continue, 'we find ourselves in Francis's situation, posing against the misery of power the joy of being' (ibid.). The outcome of this misplaced, and dangerous, analogy can only be a very peculiar understanding of the meaning of revolution in our time, 'a revolution that no power will control – because biopower and communism, cooperation and revolution remain together, in love, simplicity, and also innocence. This is the irrepressible lightness and joy of being communist' (ibid.).

So what is it that Hardt and Negri suggest? That the multitude within the empire, inspired by the example set by St Francis, should play gentle melodies on their violins to pacify the Leviathans of neoliberal globalization, just as St Francis did with the wild animals in the woods? Or that the innocent songs to life sung by the productive multitude will convince the masters of the world of their unworthiness and guilt, and hence they will give up their prerogatives, wealth and privilege? For the sake of humanity, we can only hope that these new postmodern communist activists will be somewhat more successful in defeating capitalism than the Franciscan order, and that the outcome of their activism will be more productive both in terms of the eradication of poverty and of the emancipation of mankind than that obtained long ago by the prayers and sacrifices of St Francis.

A careful reading of *Empire* allows us to conclude that the authors' goal of displaying a sophisticated analysis of the world order ends in failure. How can we explain the blindness of these two communist academics to the inherently imperialist nature of the international system? Throughout this book, I have mentioned some factors that I feel need to be taken into account in order to explain the authors' failure to achieve their goal: the extremely formalist and legalistic point of departure; the weakness of the instruments used to analyse political economy; the lack of very basic economic data; the naive acceptance of several neoliberal and postmodern axioms; the confusing heritage of structuralism and its visceral rejection of the subject; and, last but not least, the unsettling effects of a radically mistaken theory of the state.

Given the formidable intellectual calibre of Hardt and Negri, especially in the case of the Italian academic with his strong experience in the fields of Marxist social and political philosophy, how can we explain such disappointing results? In an outstanding piece of work, Terry Eagleton provides some hints that might help us solve the puzzle. In order to facilitate comprehension of his argument, Eagleton invites us to imagine the impact that an overwhelming defeat would have on a radical dissident movement, assuming that this defeat seems to erase from the public agenda the topics and proposals of the movement not only for the lifetime of its members but probably for ever. As time goes by, the movement's central theses become more characterized by their irrelevance than by their falseness. The movement's opponents no longer bother to debate or refute them, but instead they contemplate these theses with a strange combination of indifferent curiosity, 'of the same type that one can have towards the cosmology of Ptolemy or the scholastics of Thomas Aquinas' (Eagleton 1997: 17).

What are the practical alternatives that these antagonists face, given the aforementioned political and ideological catastrophe, in which a world of seemingly unmoving and objective certainties, of determinant structures, of 'laws of motion' and efficient causes, has suddenly vanished like morning fog, giving place to a colourful galaxy of social fragments, hazardous contingencies and brief circumstances whose endless combinations have led to the bankruptcy not only of Marxism but also of the whole theoretical heritage of the Enlightenment? Eagleton asserts that, for a 'postmodern sensibility', the central Marxist ideas are more often ignored than fought against: it is no longer about their wrongness, but instead, it is about their irrelevance. The Berlin Wall has already fallen; the Soviet Union has suffered a gigantic implosion, and for many today it is a blurred memory; capitalism, markets and liberal democracy seem to win everywhere, according to Francis Fukuyama; the old working class has been atomized by post-fordism; the nation-states seem to be undergoing a messy withdrawal, kneeling like serfs in front of the strength of global markets; the Warsaw Pact has been dissolved in embarrassment; social democracies shamelessly embrace neoliberalism; China opens up to foreign capital and becomes part of the WTO; and the former 'socialist camp' disappears from the international arena. What should we do?

Eagleton proposes some interesting alternatives that illuminate not only the routes probably walked by the authors, but also the itineraries covered by many of those who, in the Latin American context of the 1960s and 1970s, extolled the imminence of the revolution and awaited with their arms ready the arrival of the 'decisive day'. We can find, on the one hand, those who either cynically or sincerely moved to the right. On the other hand there are those who stayed on the left, but who did so with resignation and nostalgia, given the inexorable dissolution of their identity. There are still others who have closed their eyes in delusional triumphalism, recognizing in the weakest traces of a street demonstration or a strike clear signs of the imminent outbreak of revolution. Finally, there are those who keep their radical impulse alive, but who have had to redirect it to regions other than the political arena (ibid.).

Hardt and Negri find themselves, we could argue, within the complex field that defines this fourth alternative. They have not moved to the right, as Régis Debray or (in Latin America) Mario Vargas Llosa have done. Nor have they remained in the deep and painful perception of the defeat of a set of ideas in which they still believe, nor have they blindfolded themselves by pretending that nothing has occurred and search the planet for signs that forecast the return of the revolution. Their attitude has been healthier: opening, searching, reconstruction. Needless to say, a process of this type carries with it the inevitable risk of involuntarily accepting a premise that, in the long run, can frustrate the renovating project: the idea 'that the system is, at least for the time being, unbeatable' (ibid.). From here, a series of theoretical and practical consequences emerge that, as I will explain below, are neatly reflected in the postmodern agenda. On the one hand, an almost obsessive interest in the examination of the social forms that grow in the margins or in the interstices of the system; on the other hand, the search for those social forces that at least for now could commit some sort of transgression against the system, or could promote some type of limited and ephemeral subversion against it. The celebration of the marginal and the ephemeral, the prejudice that 'minority' is a synonym for liberation (blurring the role played by a very special minority, namely the bourgeoisie), while the massive and central, the non-marginal, is demonized, has become part of this new political and cultural ethos. If the system appears to be not only inexpugnible but also oppressive, the abandonment of a 'modern' theorization such as the Marxist one leaves no escape other than its purely imaginary negation. In this way 'the other', the different, arises as the supposed antagonist of the existing order. And it is precisely its 'otherness' that guarantees the radicalism of its antagonism, when it turns it into something impossible to assimilate and therefore into the only (illusory) alternative to the system.

The outcome of a production that is consistent with its point of departure, the invincibility of the system, is what Eagleton calls 'libertarian pessimism' (ibid.: 19). Pessimism, because the system presents itself as omnipotent and overbearing; libertarian, because it allows us to dream about multiple subversions and the overcoming of the system, without implying the identification of flesh and blood agents capable of turning those dreams into reality. The system is everywhere and it cancels the distinction between 'inside' and 'outside': whatever is inside is part of its machinery and is therefore an accomplice; whatever is outside is unable to defeat it. This is the main source of the radical pessimism that permeates this line of thought, regardless of its proclaimed revolutionary intentions.

Eagleton's work is extraordinarily suggestive and – written at the same time that Hardt and Negri were working on the writing of *Empire* – it anticipates with outstanding sharpness some of the general features present in that theorization. Like the system, the empire is omnipresent, and although the authors by no means assert that the empire is invincible, the tone used in their argument culminates with a pessimistic remark that strongly resembles capitulation. Throughout the book, the conservative forces of order are infinitely more powerful and effective than those allegedly called upon to destroy the empire. Against the powers of the bomb, the money, language and images, there arises a Third World 'hero' who instead of embracing revolution selects emigration. Moreover, the empire recognizes no 'outside' and 'inside'; we are all 'inside' and, even though this is not explicitly mentioned, we are all subjected to its arbitrary modes and its oppression. The one thing that can break it down is the unforeseeable action of the idealized 'other', the multitude, marked as it is by an infinite combination of inexhaustible singularities. The classes and the people, categories of inclusion at a time when there were still 'national' capitalism and nation-states, become volatile in the work of Hardt and Negri and they leave space for the hopeful negativity of the multitude. And some features that the authors identify as carrying a radical answer to the system – 'difference', 'hybridation', heterogeneity and inexhaustible mobility – are, as specified once again by Eagleton, 'native to the capitalist mode of production and therefore they are in no way inherently radical phenomena' (ibid.: 21).

In any case, this syndrome is far from being unique in the history of Marxism and revolutionary thought. Perry Anderson detected this with his habitual shrewdness in a relevant piece of scholarship published at a very special point in time, 1976, when Keynesian capitalism and the social-democratic strategy (followed by both socialist and communist parties, especially in Italy, France and Spain) were declining and when the first signs of the neoliberal counter-revolution were starting to show. I am referring, of course, to *Considerations on Western Marxism*, a book that was conceived to examine a different historical process, that of the 1920s and early 1930s, a period that was also deeply characterized by defeat. However, it is not my purpose here to try to reconstruct an imaginary dialogue between Eagleton and Anderson, though I believe it would be very enlightening, given the challenge that understanding the theoretical mess presented in *Empire* entails.

Defeat during the 1920s, defeat once again during the 1980s; a line of thought characteristic of that which Hannah Arendt would portray with extraordinary subtlety in her revision of the hard times undergone by the bright men and women who lived during the times that Bertolt Brecht called the 'dark ages'. A look at the lives of Rosa Luxemburg, Walter Benjamin or Bertolt Brecht himself, just to mention some of those who dedicated their lives to socialist ideals, reveals some extremely interesting teachings. For example, the fact that until the moment at which the catastrophe took place, the truth was hidden behind a thick fog of discourses, double discourses and various mechanisms that effectively concealed the ugly facts and dissipated the most reasonable doubts. Such concealment was possible thanks to the work of both public servants and good-hearted intellectuals. Then, all of a sudden, tragedy emerged (Arendt 1968: viii). Isn't it possible, then, that Hardt and Negri have become victims of the way in which intellectual production is undertaken by those who live during dark ages? There is no way for us to know. In any event, Eagleton has provided us with some clues that will help us understand the difficulties faced by left-wing intellectuals trying to explain the most abominable aspects of our time. Anderson adds some other clues that mesh very smoothly with those suggested by Eagleton. This Marxism of defeat 'has paradoxically reversed the trajectory of Marx's own intellectual development' (Anderson 1976: 52). If the founder of historical materialism turned from philosophy to politics and from politics to political economy, the 'Western Marxist' tradition reversed this path and quickly searched for a place to hide – both from revolutionary defeat at the hands of fascism and from the frustration arising from its 'triumph' and consolidation in the USSR – in the most abstruse areas of philosophy. The path of the young Marx from philosophy to politics was based on the conviction that 'the radical character of social criticism requires for us to go to a deeper level of analysis than that of the abstract man, and that in order to understand the man in context we need to delve into the anatomy of the civil society' (Boron 2000a: 302). In walking backwards in Marx's steps instead of going forwards, philosophical and epistemological thought have once again been put at the centre of the scene, overshadowing the political, economic and historical worries of the founder. This reorientation towards the philosophical and the metaphysical, clearly reflected in *Empire*, goes hand-in-hand with a second feature recognized by Anderson as one of the distinctive marks of Western Marxism in the period between the two world wars (Anderson 1976: 5). As he explains, this brand of Marxism was characterized by its esoteric language and its inaccessibility to anyone not already immersed in the field: 'The excess above and beyond the necessary verbal complexity was a sign of its divorce from any popular practice.' This conceptual proliferation becomes manifest in some symptoms that are also apparent in Hardt and Negri's work: the language is unnecessarily difficult; the syntax is, at times, impenetrable, and there is a needless use of neologisms that only contributes to a more hermetic work. Finally, there is one last element that characterizes this theoretical regression: 'Due to the lack of magnetism that the existence of a class-based social movement can provide, the Marxist tradition has leaned more and more towards the contemporary bourgeois culture.' And, Anderson suggests, 'the original relationship between Marxist theory and proletarian practice was swiftly but firmly substituted by a new relationship between Marxist theory and bourgeois theory' (ibid.: 55). The truthfulness of this assertion can be confirmed rather easily, just by taking a look at the list of authors discussed by Hardt and Negri, very few of whom have had any sort of participation in any of the big fights led by the classes and the popular sectors of society in the last twenty years.

In an interview that took place recently, Michael Hardt offered some interesting clues regarding the reasons for the astonishing theoretical involution that becomes apparent throughout *Empire*. During the interview, he observed that, in Marx's time, revolutionary thought recognized three main sources of inspiration: German philosophy, British political economy and French politics: 'Nowadays [...] the orientations have changed and revolutionary thought is guided by French philosophy, North American economic science, and Italian politics' (Hardt 2001). Hardt is right, as long as he is referring to the orientation that guided his own work and not to the sources that inspire revolutionary thought. In fact, both French philosophy and the economic theories that are taught in most business schools throughout the United States play a predominant role in *Empire*. Of course, nothing allows us to assume that these new theoretical avenues will either represent a step forwards in terms of improving and developing a theory of capitalism's imperialist stage, or, even less, that they will contribute to the elaboration of a 'guide for action' that will illuminate for us the path that the social forces of transformation and change should follow. Contrary to Hegelian dialectics, with its emphasis on the historic and transitory character of all institutions and social practices, and the contradictory character of social existence, contemporary protest seeks to update its theoretical arsenal in such unreliable sources as structuralism and post-structuralism, semiology, Lacanian psychoanalysis, and a whole series of philosophical currents characterized by their adherence to postmodernism. On the other hand, it is impossible to view the crowding-out of political economy and its replacement by North American economic science – whose narrowness, pseudo-mathematic formalism and superficiality are today universally recognized – as a step forwards towards a better understanding of the economic realities of our time. To suggest that the displacement of figures of the stature of Adam Smith or David Ricardo by pygmies such as Milton Friedman or Rudiger Dornbusch can be an encouraging sign in the construction of a leftist line of thought is, to say the least, a monumental mistake. Lastly, to say that the Italian political system, once home to the largest communist party in the western hemisphere and nowadays governed by a repulsive creature, Silvio Berlusconi, is a renewed source of inspiration that can be compared to nineteenth-century France, with its great popular uprisings and the wonderful experience of the Paris Commune, the first government of the working class in world history, demonstrates clearly the extent of this mistake, that could have disastrous consequences for both practical politics as well as in the domain of theory.

Still taking into account the aforementioned considerations, I cannot refrain from asking how it was possible for Antonio

Negri, who has written some of the most important books and articles within the Marxist tradition over the last quarter of a century, to write a book in which it appears as if he has forgotten everything that he had previously thought. There is no doubt that Negri has been one of the most important Marxist theorists.[1] Born in Padua, Italy, in 1933, he graduated in Philosophy from his natal city's university, and in the 1960s was appointed Professor of Theory of the State in the Political Science department in Padua. At the same time, his practical involvement in Italian political life turned him into one of the leaders of the Potere Operaio and one of the most outstanding figures of the Italian left, very critical of the political and theoretical line fostered by the Italian Communist Party, PCI. In 1979 Negri was arrested and sent to prison after a faulty legal process. He was accused of being the intellectual mentor of the terrorist actions of the Red Brigades, including the assassination of Italian Prime Minister Aldo Moro. In 1983 the Italian Radical Party, a moderate combination of liberalism and social democracy, sponsored his candidacy to parliament, in order to pressure the Italian government into revising the legal sentence. After being elected member of parliament by popular vote, parliamentary immunity allowed him to get out of prison. Shortly after, the ruling party with a majority in parliament – with the infamous complicity of PCI MPs, in a scandalous political act – revoked his immunity, and, as many other anti-fascists had done before, Negri departed for exile in France. The already entirely corrupt Italian judicial system declared Negri a rebel and he was condemned to thirty years in prison, accused of 'armed insurrection against the state' with an additional sentence of four and a half years because of his 'moral responsibility' for violent confrontations between the police, students and workers that took place in Milan between 1973 and 1977.

---

1 A subtle analysis of Negri's intellectual and political trajectory is to be found in Callinicos (2003).

Imprisonment did not prevent Negri from writing; among texts written in prison, *La Anomalia Salvaje*, published in 1981, is worth mentioning. By this time he had already published some of his main contributions to Marxist theory: *Operai e Stato. Fra Rivoluzione d'ottobre e New Deal* (1972), *Crisi dello stato-piano* (1974), *Proletari e Stato* (1976), *La Forma Stato. Per la Critica dell'Economia Politica della Constituzione* (1977), *Marx oltre Marx* (1979), and a seminal article about capitalist restructuring after the great depression, 'Keynes and the Capitalist theory of the State', originally published in Italy and later translated into several languages and reprinted in *Labor of Dionysus*, a book that Negri wrote years later with Michael Hardt. Negri remained in France for fourteen years, between 1983 and 1997. François Mitterrand's government's protection was decisive in terms of dissuading the Italian secret service from its original intention of kidnapping Negri. During his years in France, Negri taught at the famous École Normale Supérieure and at the University of Paris VIII and, together with other distinguished French colleagues, he founded a new theoretical magazine: *Futur Antérieur*. It is obvious that during his stay in France Negri shelved his interest in German philosophy and acquired a great familiarity with French philosophical debates marked by the presence of intellectuals such as Louis Althusser, Alain Badiou, Étienne Balibar, Jean Baudrillard, Gilles Deleuze, Jacques Derrida, Michel Foucault, Félix Guattari, Jacques Lacan, Jean-Françoise Lyotard, Jacques Rancière and many others. His stay in France was a period of intense theoretical production and profound intellectual, and to some extent political, reorientation. Among the most important books published during that period it is worth mentioning *Les nouveaux espaces de liberté*, in collaboration with Félix Guattari (1985); *Fabbriche del soggetto* (1987); *The Politics of Subversion* (1989); *Il potere constituente* (1992); and *Labor of Dionysus: A Critique of the State-form*, co-authored with Michael Hardt (1994). In 1997, after the scandalous collapse of the Italian state institutions and the crises of Christian Democracy and the Italian Socialist Party, Negri returned to Italy where his previous sentence had been revoked. He spent a short period in the Rebibbia prison and, afterwards, was permitted to serve a new, shorter and more benign sentence that entails living at home in Trastevere during the day and spending the nights in prison. It is in this context that Negri co-authored *Empire*, with Michael Hardt

8 The persistence of imperialism

'The United States seem to be destined by Providence to plague the Americas with misery in the name of freedom' *Simon Bolívar*

The radical goal repeatedly declared throughout *Empire* – to contribute to the creation of a 'general theoretical structure and for that structure to constitute a set of conceptual tools allowing us to theorize and act in the Empire and against it' – falls to earth as a result of the incurable weakness of the analysis. Unfortunately, the toolbox is lacking some of the most basic instruments for theorizing about the empire and, more seriously, for fighting against it. This final critique could be summarized by saying that the book's most crucial fault is its serious diagnostic mistakes. There is no connection between a theoretical background that is unarguably conservative in nature – or whose nature is at best confusing – and which derives mainly from conventional neoliberal knowledge that extols globalization and 'naturalizes' capitalism on one hand, and the blurry vision of a new society and a new international order to be built over radically different premises on the other. If the diagnosis is inaccurate, the new social and political construction is doomed to failure. The fragility of the analysis is apparent as early as the Preface of the book. The authority cited in order to define the fundamental concept that gives the book its name is not Lenin or Bukharin or Luxemburg or, more recently, Samir Amin, André Gunder Frank, Immanuel Wallerstein, Eric Hobsbawm, Samuel Eisenstadt, Pablo González Casanova, Agustin Cueva, Alonso Aguilar, Helio Jaguaribe, John Saxe-Fernández, James Petras or any of the many other scholars who have contributed to our understanding of the topic. No. Instead, the authors mention Maurice Duverger, a French political scientist comfortably installed in the most conventional currents within the discipline and an academic who has never been associated with any of the critical schools of thought. These limitations are even more conspicuous when it becomes clear how easily the authors present as their own the conventional definitions used by business school professors who conceive globalization as an 'irresistible and irreversible' process before which the democratic states should kneel. We can recognize in this formulation the old trap of the bourgeois ideologists for whom capitalism is nothing but the 'natural' manifestation of our human acquisitive and egoistic impulses, and every system other than capitalism is viewed as 'artificial' or as the imprudent product of political will. Hardt and Negri appear to have paid no attention to the sensible comments made by a genuine American liberal not too long ago: John K. Galbraith, who sharply argued that 'globalization is not a serious concept. Us, Americans, have invented it in order to hide our policies of economic penetration in the rest of the world' (Galbraith 1997: 2). This argument comes very close to admitting that capitalism's irresistibility and irreversibility leave no alternative options, an argument deeply engrained in the heart of neoliberal thought. Ellen Meiskins Wood (2003: 63) is right when she observes that if 'there is no material point at which the power of capital can be challenged, and with all forms of political action effectively disabled, the rule of capital is complete and eternal'.

The clamorous inconsistency between the authors' analysis and their political goals is also revealed when the reader asks to what extent the system's 'global logic' is overlaid by contradictions that could eventually lead to its collapse and to the preparation of the material and cultural bases needed to build an alternative system. This is particularly serious when we realize that the authors seem not to be aware of the fundamental continuity that exists between the supposedly 'new' empire's global logic, its fundamental actors, its institutions, norms, rules and procedures, and the logic that existed in the allegedly dead phase of imperialism. Hardt and Negri seem not to have realized that the strategic actors are the same, the large transnational companies but with a national base, on one hand, and the governments of industrialized countries, on the other hand; that the decisive institutions are still those that characterized the imperialist phase they claim is now finished, such as the IMF, the World Bank, the WTO, and other similar organizations; and that the rules of the game of the international system are still the ones dictated mainly by the United States and global neoliberalism, and that were imposed by force during the climax of the neoliberal counter-revolution through the 1980s and the beginning of the 1990s. Given their design, purpose and functions, these rules do nothing but continuously reproduce and perpetuate the old imperialist structure in a new guise. We would be much closer to the truth if, paraphrasing Lenin, we say that the empire is the 'superior stage' of imperialism and nothing else. Its functioning logic is the same, and so are the ideology that justifies its existence, the actors that make its dynamics, and the unfair results that reveal the persistence of relations of oppression and exploitation. In Marx's analyses, the contradictions in the development of bourgeois society would lead it to its own destruction. The logic of social development was presided over by class struggles and contradictions between the forces of production and the social relations of production. The problem with Hardt and Negri's analyses is that the new global logic of rule that allegedly prevails in the empire as imagined by the authors lacks any structural or inherent contradictions.[1]

The only contradiction that is present is that of the potential threat posed by the multitude if it ever abandoned the lethargy

1 For a penetrating analysis of the shortcomings of the 'classic theories of imperialism' and the new challenges posed by today's new facets of imperialism, see Panitch and Gindin (2004) and, in general, the articles included in *Socialist Register 2004* (Panitch and Leys 2004). See also John Bellamy Foster (2002).

in which it is kept by the mass media and the bourgeois cultural industry. Even if this happened, though, there is nothing in the book to convince the reader of the existence of structural – and hence impossible to overcome – contradictions between the empire and the multitude. On the contrary, it would be possible to extend the authors' argument to say that if the rulers behave wisely, they are in a very good position to absorb the demands of the multitude by means of relaxing migratory norms or progressively establishing a guaranteed minimum income. Episodes during which the dominant classes have been forced to adopt progressive policies so as to hold back popular tides or in order to co-opt potential adversaries have not been infrequent in the political history of the twentieth century, and the two measures mentioned above are in no way incompatible with the survival of the capitalist relations of production nor are they incompatible with the continuity of imperialism.

During the 1980s, neoliberalism won a strategic battle for the meanings of words used in everyday speech, particularly in the public sphere. Throughout the globe the word 'reform' was successfully used to refer to events that a somewhat rigorous analysis would have undoubtedly classified as 'counter-reform'. The aforementioned 'reforms' were materialized in not too reformist policies such as the dismantling of social security, the reduction of social provisions, the cuts in public spending on education, health and housing, and the legalization of the oligopolistic control of the economy. The word 'deregulation' was actively promoted by the neoliberal and managerial ideologists cited throughout *Empire* to refer to a process through which governmental intervention in economic matters was suppressed in order to restore the 'natural self-regulation' of economic processes. In fact, what 'deregulation' means is that the previous regulations established by democratic governments – and which led, in some way, to a certain degree of popular sovereignty – were banished, and after this happened the capacity to regulate the functioning of markets was left in the hands of the most powerful actors, the oligopolies. Governmental capacity to regulate was privatized and transferred to large companies. As Samir Amin wrote, 'all the markets are regulated, and they only function under that condition. The essential thing is to know who regulates them and how' (Amin 2001: 26). To conclude: the commonsense of the last two decades of the previous century has been saturated by the contents of neoliberal ideology. Further proof of this fact is the ready acceptance of the dogma claiming that state-owned companies were by definition inefficient and produced low-quality goods and services; that the state was a bad administrator: that private companies satisfy the demands and requirements of consumers; that oligopolies promote social progress through unrestricted market freedom; and, finally, that, as argued in the 'trickle-down' theory, if the rich get richer, the wealth concentrated at the top of the social pyramid soons spills over to reach the least advantaged sectors of the population. Nowadays, all those stories face a terminal crisis of credibility.

For a long time, the hegemony of neoliberalism was not only economic and ideological but also political. In that field too we observe a backwards movement. Economies do not respond as predicted and, after more than twenty years of painful experiments, the results are dire. Argentina is just the most recent case, but in no way the only one, that demonstrates once more the final result of the policies promoted by the Washington Consensus. The political formulas of a successful neoliberalism, whose archetypes are still the sinister figures of Carlos S. Menem in Argentina, Carlos Salinas de Gortari in Mexico and Alberto Fujimori in Peru, have demonstrated their inability to remain in power and their inability to establish a new structure of domination in accordance with the needs of the empire's dominant classes. The ideological hegemony of neoliberalism; its capacity to ascribe new and contradictory meanings to old words, is being rapidly eroded. *Empire* could perfectly be thought of as a late chapter of that history. The book was published in 2000 and its real function – I concede this was not the intention of the authors – seems to have been to make a little bit more palatable the increasingly atrocious and despicable features of the imperialism of the end of the century. Probably nothing could have been more convenient for the imperialist powers, guided not without friction and contradictions by the United States, than this representation of the imperialist order metamorphosed into a phantasmagoric system, without identifiable dominators and beneficiaries, and, above all, inspired by the most elevated legal notions of Kantian lineage that only the enemies of freedom and justice would dare to criticize. While the authors were giving the last touch to their metaphysical empire, the imperialists were eager to launch the Colombia Plan with its declared goal of stabilizing the political and military situation in that country and of controlling drug traffic in the area, whose funds are carefully laundered in fiscal havens throughout the region that survive thanks to Washington's indulgence. Another of the aforementioned project's objectives is the establishment of a strategic base in the heart of South America as a means to monitor the advances of the popular movement in Brazil, a country which, by chance, is the home of two of the most important popular organizations of the western world, the PT and the MST. Another important imperialist initiative is the Puebla/Panama Plan intended to 'solve' the (apparently incommunicable, according to Hardt and Negri) conflict in Chiapas and, in addition, to set up an establishment in the largest Mexican reservoir of fresh water in order to provide Southern California with that vital liquid. Moreover, it was imperialism that launched a 'humanitarian intervention' in the former Yugoslavia; it constantly sabotages the construction of Mercosur so as to facilitate the rapid formal 'integration' of the Latin American economies into American hegemony through the Free Trade Area of the Americas (FTAA); and it works without ceasing to ensure the collaboration of some regional governments, such as those of Argentina, Costa Rica and Uruguay, in imposing sanctions on Cuba for alleged human rights violations and to make it pay an exorbitant price for its lack of docility towards American imperialism. In other latitudes, its activism leads it to support its allies in Turkey when they commit genocide against the Kurdish minority without fear, and to support similar actions by Indonesia against East Timor, and by the fascist Israeli government of Ariel Sharon against the Palestinians. A few years earlier, the empire, allegedly in the name of universal law, invaded Panama, killing thousands of innocent civilians with the goal of capturing President Noriega, a former collaborator of the CIA and the DEA, and put in power by Washington; it caused more than 30,000 deaths in its offensive against the Sandinista government in Nicaragua; and it started the Gulf War. In the economic terrain, imperialism was again active, promoting the approval of the Multilateral Agreement on Investments, in order to legalize the tyranny of markets, especially in the Third World, and it made strong efforts to ensure that the IMF and the World Bank would not lend a nickel to those countries that did not accept the 'conditionalities' imposed by the market's international financial institutions. In this way, a recent loan to Ecuador included around a hundred and forty requirements of this type – among them, massive dismissals of public servants, cuts in public social spending, an end to subsidies – and more than two hundred 'conditionalities' were reported in several loans to sub-Saharan Africa, all of which were oriented to consolidate the presence of 'market forces' in the economy. On the other hand, imperialism has been constantly imposing economic policies that severely undermine the economic sovereignty of countries in the periphery and diminish their likelihood of being able to develop their economies, consolidate their democracies, and respond positively to their populations' expectations of material and spiritual progress (Stiglitz 2000). Leo Panitch claims, with regard to this issue, that a report by the World Bank demonstrates that on the same year in which the MIA was aborted 'there were at least as many as 151 changes in the regulations that govern direct foreign investments in 76 countries, and 89% of them were favorable to foreign capital' (Panitch 2000: 16). Meanwhile, Pablo González Casanova has developed a methodology for the study of the surplus transferences from the Third World towards metropolitan capitalism. In the twenty-three years from 1972 to 1995, the volume of those transfers hoovered up by the empire's dominant classes reached the astonishing amount of $4.5 trillion; the calculations made using this same methodology exclusively for Latin America by Saxe-Fernández and Núñes show that the figure 'surpasses the 2 trillion dollar threshold paid in two decades of globalizing neo-liberalism, a magnitude that is equal to the combined GDPs of all the countries in Latin America and the Caribbean in 1997' (González Casanova 1998; Saxe Fernández et al. 2001: 105, 111).

In a word, imperialist oppression continues to exist while a lost patrol of radical scholars proclaims that the age of imperialism has concluded and exalts the figure of St Francis as the paradigm of the renovated militancy against the spectre of an empire that is impossible to seize, define or find, and hence impossible to beat. That which is openly recognized by scholars of imperialism such as Brzezinski and Huntington, magically disappears from the 'radical critical' vision of the empire. Meanwhile, approximately 100,000 people die each day in the periphery due to hunger, malnutrition and curable diseases, because of the uninterrupted continuity of the exactions of this 'smooth space across which subjectivities glide', which the authors call empire, a non-imperialist regime that day after day produces a silent bloodbath that the bourgeois media take pains to conceal. These people die without receiving the most elementary medical care. Each year a country of the size of Spain, Argentina or Colombia is wiped off the face of the earth in the name of the despicable 'new international economic order', an order that, if we are to believe in Hardt and Negri, has ceased to be imperialist.

Hardt and Negri's stubbornness in defending their mistaken conceptions has become stronger since the first publication of their book. In an interview with *Le Monde Diplomatique*, Negri insisted on his view that the empire lacks any national base and that it is the expression of the international order created by 'collective capital' once it emerged victorious from the long civil war waged against the workers throughout the twentieth century. 'Contrary to what the last supporters of nationalism sustain, the empire is not North American; in addition, throughout the history of the United States they have been much less imperialist than the British, the French, the Russians, or the Dutch' (Negri 2001: 13). According to Negri, the empire's beneficiaries are certainly American capitalists, but also their European counterparts, those magnates who built their fortunes within the Russian Mafia and all the wealthy in the Arab world, Asia, Africa or Latin America, who send their children to Harvard and their money to Wall Street. Clearly, in this pseudo-totality of the empire and in its unbearable emptiness, not only is there no theoretical space in which to distinguish between exploiters and exploited but also there is no room to conceive the dominant coalition as anything different from an undifferentiated gang of capitalists. In this way, and departing from this analytical sterility, 'collective capital' produces the miracle of controlling the world economy (the reader should be reminded that only 200 transnational mega-corporations, 96 per cent of which have their headquarters in just eight countries, have a combined volume of sales that is higher than the GDP of all the countries in the globe except the nine largest ones) without structures, organizations, institutions, hierarchies, agents, rules or norms.[2] In addition, if any conflict

2 We add: the annual income of Exxon is almost equal to Australia's GDP; that of Ford is similar to Denmark's GDP; that of the British-Dutch oil company Shell is almost double the GDP of one of the largest oil producers in the world, Venezuela. General Motors has an annual income that exceeds the combined GDP of Ireland, New Zealand and Hungary (Restivo 2002: 24–5).

took place within it, such a conflict would be merely accidental or circumstantial, and it would be easily solved by appealing to the good-will of the parties concerned. All of a sudden the world order created by North American hegemony during the post-war era disappears in front of our eyes, and the magnates of the Russian Mafia seem to have the same weight and relevance as their North American counterparts. The main institutions which model the international imperialist order – the IMF, the World Bank, the WTO, NATO, the OECD and other similar institutions – seem to bear no more relation to Washington than they do to Osama Bin Laden's family or to any other Arab magnate, although the organic intellectuals of the empire insist on characterizing them as an informal part of the North American government. In this phantasmagoric view of the empire, the 'conditionalities' of the international financial institutions would be dictated by an Arab millionaire, a Portuguese banker, a Japanese whaler, a Latin American oligarch and, of course, an American businessman. In the same way, the erratic movements of the United Nations are the result of a fight between the aforementioned subjects. It is not necessary to be an international relations expert to demonstrate the falsehood of this argument. Recent events in Venezuela (the failed coup d'etat against Hugo Chávez in April 2002) dissipate any doubt regarding the persistent oppressive presence of imperialism. A coup that the CIA had been preparing for more than a year, and which was blessed, in a sign of arrogance close to sheer stupidity, hours after its occurrence by the presidential spokesman at the White House (violating the Organization of American States' resolutions that Washington had promoted when it had been convenient for it to do so), and which immediately had the 'disinterested' collaboration of the IMF that, surprisingly and without anybody having to ask for it, offered its help to the new government at a time when it had been recognized only by the United States and its European footman, José M. Aznar, the situation still not having been resolved. This behaviour by the IMF proves once again that this 'multilateral organization' is, in reality, a minor department inside the White House.

This record completely invalidates Negri's statement made during a recent interview in which he expanded on the issues developed in *Empire*: 'We think that there is no centralization place within the empire, and that it is necessary to speak of a non-place. We are not claiming that Washington is not important: Washington has the bomb. New York has the dollar. Los Angeles has the language and the means of communication' (Albiac 2002: 2).

No further comment.

Epilogue

Fame and celebrity have rarely gone hand-in-hand with critical thinking. The history of political philosophy teaches us that adversarial spirits have usually been persecuted and silenced by the dominant classes. In most cases, this has been achieved by means of more or less brutal coercion. Antonio Negri has been, for almost thirty years, a victim of this methodology: his militancy in Italian social struggles, as well as his significant contributions to both political theory and political philosophy – two fields also marked by the ups and downs of class struggles – brought down on him the fury of the Italian bourgeoisie and its political representatives, and it also brought persecution, incarceration and exile. On other, less frequent, occasions, those who contest the existing social order are faced only with the indifference of the powerful. This occurs when the dominant groups find themselves in such a safe position and are so confident of the stability of their own supremacy that they allow themselves the luxury of practising the art of tolerance. Needless to say, this exercise is practised only on condition that the dissident voices can be heard only by a small circle of harmless followers who lack any organic link with civil society, and who, for that reason, are incapable of becoming a serious threat to the dominant classes. Given this, how can we explain the 'unlimited praise' that, according to John Bellamy Foster, was heaped on two leftist scholars – namely Michael Hardt and Antonio Negri – in some of the most select intellectual bastions of the bourgeoisie, such as the *New York Times*, *Time* magazine and the *Observer* of London, to which I could add a newspaper linked to the most reactionary factions of Argentine capitalism, *La Nación* (Bellamy Foster 2001).

In concluding this examination the answer seems to be clear:

the favourable reception given by the establishment's mandarins to *Empire* shows that they read the book carefully, that they correctly understood its most profound message, and that they accurately concluded that there was nothing within the book that could be considered incompatible with the dominant ideology or with the self-image that the powerful like to exhibit. Although the metaphysical radicalism of its narrative and its abstruse allusions to the contradictions of capitalism did not cease to irritate the most intolerant and narrow-minded intellectuals of the empire, the main argument shows a surprising and welcome similarity to the main thesis that the ideologists of 'globalization' have been promoting around the world since the 1980s, namely: that the nation-state is practically dead, that a global logic rules the world, and that defying this abominable structure, whose concrete beneficiaries as well as its victims and oppressed are lost in the shadows, there is a new and amorphous entity, the 'multitude', no longer the people, let alone the workers or the proletariat. Regardless of the repeated invocations to communism and the good society that make the imperial energumens shiver, *Empire* leaves the reader without answers as to why the men and women of the empire should rebel, against whom, and how to create a new type of society. Although *Empire* formally criticizes capitalism as an inhuman, oppressive, exploitative and unfair mode of production, it vanishes in the translucent air of postmodernity. It becomes, in a manner of speaking, invisible, just like American imperialism, and in this way both are 'naturalized'. Hunger, poverty, death, wars, diseases and the whole catalogue of human miseries that were observed throughout the twentieth century are rhetorically transformed in dull and almost impenetrable phraseology that, in spite of the manifest intentions of its creators, hides the most despicable features of neoliberal globalization and of contemporary capitalism.

For the reasons displayed throughout my book, I find it highly unlikely that the anti-imperialist fighters of the world will find in *Empire* any realistic and persuasive argument to illuminate their path or to help them understand what is happening in the world. More likely, a 'counsel of surrender would be the message of a manifesto on behalf of global capital. It is also, like it or not, the message of Michael Hardt and Antonio Negri's *Empire*' (Meiskins Wood 2003: 63). Given its mistakes and confusions, it is easy to understand why the book was acclaimed as a true revelation by some of the world's most important mass media tightly associated with the imperialist structure that overwhelms us. In any case, it is good to know that, as Hannah Arendt reminded us, 'even in the darkest night we still have the right to wait for some illumination', and that this will probably come not from a colourful conceptual and theoretical apparatus but from the small lights that will emanate from the initiatives that men and women adopt in order to put an end to, in Marx's words, this painful and barbarian 'pre-history' of humanity finally to enter a superior stage of civilization (Arendt 1968: ix). I want to believe, going back to Hardt and Negri's work, that the mistakes that we have identified in *Empire* will be rectified in a new study undertaken by these authors. In Negri's case I am inclined to think that the mistakes detected in this book could be due to distortions produced by a long exile, even if it is in Paris; to the lack of ability to travel around the world and to confirm, with his own eyes, the sinister realities of imperialism; and finally, to the rarefied intellectual Parisian atmosphere, whose provincialism and splendid self-reference were repeatedly underlined by notable French intellectuals such as Jean-Paul Sartre, or others residing in France like Nicos Poulantzas. Negri's contributions to the development of social and political Marxist theory do not deserve such a disappointing ending. I hope with all my heart to have, in the short term, the satisfaction of commenting, in completely different terms, on a new book in which Negri's extraordinary talent meets again with his own history.

Bibliography

Ahmad, A. (2004) 'Imperialism of Our Time', in L. Panitch and C. Leys (eds), *Socialist Register 2004* (London: Merlin Press).

Albiac, G. (2002) 'El comunismo al día', in *Radar*, supplement, *Página/12* (Buenos Aires) 30, March.

Amin, S. (1974) *Accumulation on a World Scale* (New York: Monthly Review Press).

— (1992) *Empire of Chaos* (New York: Monthly Review Press).

— (1997) *Capitalism in the Age of Globalization* (London and New Jersey: Zed Books).

— (2001) *El hegemonismo de los Estados Unidos y el Desvanecimiento del Proyecto Europeo* (Madrid: El Viejo Topo).

Anderson, P. (1976) *Considerations on Western Marxism* (London: New Left Books).

— (2004) 'The Role of Ideas in the Construction of Alternatives', in A. A. Boron (ed.), *New Worldwide Hegemony. Alternatives for Change and Social Movements* (Buenos Aires: CLACSO).

Arendt, H. (1968) *Men in Dark Times* (San Diego, CA: Harcourt Brace).

Arrighi, G. (1995) *The Long Twentieth Century* (London: Verso).

Balakrishnan, G. (ed.) (2003) *Debating Empire* (London: Verso).

Barlow, M. (1998) 'Creeping Corporativism. Every Cultural Institution is in Jeopardy', *The Bulletin* (Toronto), 51 (12).

Bellamy Foster, J. (2001) 'Imperialism and "Empire"', *Monthly Review*, 53 (7), December.

— (2002) 'The Rediscovery of Imperialism', *Monthly Review*, 54 (6), November.

Boron, A. A. (1995) *State, Capitalism and Democracy in Latin America* (Boulder, CO: Lynne Rienner).

— (1997) *Estado, Capitalismo y Democracia en América Latina* (Buenos Aires: EUDEBA/CBC).

— (2000a) (ed.) *Filosofía Política Moderna* (Buenos Aires: CLACSO).

— (2000b) *Tras el Búho de Minerva. Mercado contra democracia en el capitalismo de fin de siglo* (Buenos Aires: Fondo de Cultura Económica).

— (2001a) 'El nuevo orden imperial y cómo desmontarlo', in J. Seoane and E. Taddei (eds), *Resistencias Mundiales. De Seattle a Porto Alegre* (Buenos Aires: CLACSO).

— (2001b) 'La selva y la polis. Interrogantes en torno a la teoría política del Zapatismo', *Chiapas* (Mexico), 12.

— (2002) *Tras el Búho de Minerva. Mercado contra democracia en el capitalismo de fin de siglo* (Buenos Aires: CLACSO).

Boron, A. A., J. Gambina and N. Minsburg (eds) (1999) *Tiempos Violentos. Neoliberalismo, globalización y desigualdad en América Latina* (Buenos Aires: CLACSO/EUDEBA).

Bowles, S. and H. Gintis (1982) 'The Crisis of Liberal Democratic Capitalism: The Case of United States', *Politics and Society*, II (1), pp. 51–93.

— (1986) *Democracy and Capitalism: Property, Community, and the Contradictions of Modern Social Thought* (New York: Basic Books).

Brzezinski, Z. (1998) *El Gran Tablero Mundial: la superioridad norteamericana y los imperativos geoestratégicos* (Buenos Aires: Paidós).

Bull, M. (2003) 'You Can't Build a New Society with a Stanley Knife', in G. Balakrishnan (ed.), *Debating Empire* (London: Verso), pp. 83–96.

Callinicos, A. (2003) 'Toni Negri in Perspective', in G. Balakrishnan (ed.), *Debating Empire* (London: Verso), pp. 121–43.

Cangi, A. (2002) 'Pequeño saltamontes', *Radar*, supplement, *Página/12* (Buenos Aires), 31 March.

Cardoso, O. R. (2003) 'La Argentina no sabe qué hacer con su burguesía', interview with Toni Negri, *Zona,* supplement to *Clarín* newspaper (Buenos Aires), 26 October.

Chomsky, N. (1993) *Year 501. The Conquest Continues* (Boston, MA: South End Press).

— (1994) *World Orders, Old and New* (London: Pluto Press).

— (1998) *Noam Chomsky habla de América Latina* (Buenos Aires: Editorial 21).

— (2000a) 'Poder en el escenario global', *New Left Review* (Madrid, Spanish edn), January, pp. 232–62.

— (2000b) 'Una entrevista con Noam Chomsky', in A. A. Boron, *Tras el Búho de Minerva. Mercado contra democracia en el capitalismo de fin de siglo* (Buenos Aires: Fondo de Cultura Económica).

— (2001) *El terror como política exterior de los Estados Unidos (*Buenos Aires: Libros del Zorzal).

— (2003a) *Hegemony or Survival. America's Quest for Global Dominance* (New York: Metropolitan Books).

— (2003b) 'Dilemmas of Domination', in A. A. Boron (ed.), *New Worldwide Hegemony. Alternatives for Change and Social Movements* (Buenos Aires: CLACSO).

Cox, R. W. (1986) 'Social Forces, States and World Orders: Beyond International Relations Theory', in R. O. Keohane, *Neorealism and its Critics* (New York: Columbia University Press).

— (1987) *Production, Power, and World Order. Social Forces in the Making of History* (New York, Columbia University Press).

Cueva, A. (1986) 'La democracia en América Latina: "¿Novia del socialismo o concubina del imperialismo?"', *Estudios Latinoamericanos*, Vol. 1(1), July/December (Mexico), CELA/FCPyS, UNAM, pp. 49–54.

Dahl, R. A. (1995) *A Preface to Economic Democracy* (Berkeley and Los Angeles: University of California Press).

de Sousa Santos, B. (1999) *Reinventar la Democracia. Reinventar el Estado* (Madrid: Ediciones Sequitur).

de Tocqueville, A. (1969) *Democracy in America* (Garden City, NY: Anchor Books).

Drucker, P. F. (1997) 'The Global Economy and the Nation-State', *Foreign Affairs*, 76 (5), September/October, pp. 159–71.

Duarte-Plon, L. (2004) 'An Interview with Antonio Negri', *Le Passant Ordinaire*, 27 July.

Eagleton, T. (1997) 'Where Do Postmodernists Come from?" in E. Meiskins Wood and J. Bellamy Foster (eds), *In Defense of History* (New York: Monthly Review Press).

Friedman, Thomas L. (1999) 'A Manifesto for the Fast World', *New York Times*, 28 March.

Galbraith, J. K. (1997) 'Entrevista a John K. Galbraith', *Folha de São Paulo* (Brazil), 2 November, pp. 2–13.

González Casanova, P. (1998) *La explotación global* (México: CEIICH/ UNAM).

Gramsci, A. (1971) *Selections from the Prison Notebooks* (New York: International Publishers).

Hardt, M. (2001) 'El laboratorio italiano' (mimeo).

Hardt, M. and A. Negri (2000) *Empire* (Cambridge, MA: Harvard University Press). Translated into Spanish: *Imperio* (Buenos Aires: Paidós, 2002).

Huntington, S. P. (1999) 'The Lonely Superpower', *Foreign Affairs*, 78 (2).

Kapstein, E. (1991/92) 'We Are Us: The Myth of the Multinational', *The National Interest* (Winter).

Lander, E. (1998) 'El Acuerdo Multilateral de Inversiones (MIA). El capital diseña una constitución universal', *Revista Venezolana de Economía y Ciencias Sociales* (Caracas), 2–3, April/September.

Lukács, G. (1971) *History and Class Consciousness* (Cambridge, MA: MIT Press).

Meiskins Wood, E. (1995) *Democracy against Capitalism. Renewing Historical Materialism* (Cambridge: Cambridge University Press).

— (2000) 'Trabajo, clase y estado en el capitalismo global', *Observatorio Social de América Latina* (Buenos Aires: CLACSO), 1, June, pp. 111–18.

— (2003) 'A Manifesto for Global Capital', in G. Balakrishnan (ed.), *Debating Empire* (London: Verso), pp. 61–82.

Negri, A. (1991) 'J. M. Keynes y la teoría capitalista del estado en el '29', *El Cielo por Asalto* (Buenos Aires), I (2), pp. 97–118.

— (2001) 'The Empire after Imperialism, *Le Monde Diplomatique*, January.

Panitch, L. (2000) 'The New Imperial State', *New Left Review*, 2, March/April, pp. 5–20.

Panitch, L. and S. Gindin (2004) 'Global Capitalism and the American Empire', in L. Panitch and C. Leys (eds), *Socialist Register 2004* (London: Merlin Press), pp. 1–42.

Panitch, L. and C. Leys (eds) (2004) *Socialist Register 2004* (London: Merlin Press).

Restivo, N. (2002) 'Entre las 100 economías mas grandes, 51 son multi-nacionales', *Clarín* (Buenos Aires), 17 March.

Ruigrock, W. and R. Van Tulder (1995) *The Logic of International Restructuring* (London: Routledge).

Rustin, M. (2003) 'A Postmodern Theory of Revolution', in G. Balakrishnan (ed.), *Debating Empire* (London: Verso), pp. 1–18.

Sastre, A. (2003) *La batalla de los intelectuales. O nuevo discurso de las armas y las letras* (Euskal Herría: Editorial Hiru).

Saxe-Fernández, J., J. Petras, H. Veltmeyer and O. Núñez (2001) *Globalización, Imperialismo y Clase Social* (Buenos Aires and Mexico City: Grupo Editorial Lumen/Humanitas).

Stiglitz, J. (2000) 'What I Learned at the World Economic Crisis', *New Republic*, 17 April.

Strange, S. (1986) *Casino Capitalism* (Oxford: Blackwell).

— (1989) 'Towards a Theory of Transnational Empire', in E.-O. Czempiel and J. Rosenau (eds), *Global Changes and Theoretical Challenge. Approaches to World Politics for the 1990's* (Lexington, VA: Lexington Books).

— (1998) *Mad Money. When Markets Outgrow Governments* (Ann Arbor, MI: University of Michigan Press).

Tilly, C. (2003) 'A Nebulous Empire', in G. Balakrishnan (ed.), *Debating Empire* (London: Verso), pp. 26–8.

United Nations Development Program (UNDP) *Human Development Report*, annual publication (New York: United Nations).

Vidal, G. (2002) *Perpetual War for Perpetual Peace* (New York: Thunder's Mouth Press/Nation Books)

Wallerstein, I. (1974) *The Modern World System*, Vol. 1 (New York: Academic Books).

— (1980) *The Modern World System*, Vol. 2 (New York: Academic Books).

— (1988) *The Modern World System*, Vol. 3 (New York: Academic Books).

— (1995) *After Liberalism* (New York: New Press).

Weiss, L. (1997) 'Globalization and the Myth of the Powerless States', *New Left Review*, 225, September/October.

Wresch, W. (1996) *Disconnected. Haves and Have-nots in the Information Age* (New Brunswick, NJ: Rutgers University Press).

Index of proper names

General index